FOREWORD

Those that know the genuine America, especially those that lived in America during 2020 were dispirited.

ll Americans heard in the established press for a really long time is the means by which awful America is, and was, and how America is "terrible."

- When we see police killing unarmed black men we wonder.
- When we see how a government supports and props up Wall Street and creates an enormous wealth disparity, we wonder.
- When we see homeless people sleeping in the streets, we wonder.
- When we see dominant monopolistic social media platforms censor the thoughts and ideas of only one side of an argument, we wonder.
- When we see reports of increased drug overdoses, and suicides, and "deaths of despair" spiking, we wonder.
- When we see riots and looting and violence, we wonder more.

Is America bad?

When we return in history

- When we see how Columbus killed natives and took slaves, we wonder.
- When we see how white settlers took the land from Native Americans, we wonder.
- When we see how Blacks were taken from Africa and brought here against their will and pressed into service and slavery, we wonder.
- When we see how naturalized Japanese American citizens were interred into concentration camps, we wonder.

There ain't no real way to gloss over all of this. This is for sure awful. Presently, despite what some may say, assuming there are a few wrongs happening in America today, the fights may really be something to be thankful for. Fights work for change or improvement and are an intrinsically ensured right.

owever, as these fights become vicious, crowd like, and wild, the terrible side of human instinct uncovers itself.

The rough horde, that introduced itself as "great and upright" appeared as awful and as malevolent as the causes they came to look for equity for.

Whether these hordes were co-picked (or taken over by others that were more extremist) it was evident that things went excessively far with the out breaks of plundering, viciousness, and revolting, and absolutely no part of this was to anybody's greatest advantage. Those crowds that obliterate, and fury, and consume, and rage some more, are alarming. These crowds were furious, disdain filled and bigoted. Pardon nobody! No pardoning! No prudence! No point of view, simply fury, plunder, and burn!

For those causes those protestors came to "fight" about things, one could ask, were those underlying issues "America's" fault?

… .or that current, or past government's fault?

… or is this the shortcoming of a couple of misinformed people living in America during those occasions that serious those violations. Is it their fault?

guess we can fault all issues or offenses of the past on white individuals… especially guys… who live at this very moment and fault everything on them and make them PAY for the wrongdoings of others that appeared as though them, only dependent on their skin color.

Yeah, that is justice.

There is an individual of color… I mean a white man… lets lynch him and make him PAY for the violations of the others!

… ..better

believe it,

equity. Or on

the other hand

not

What was intriguing with regards to the crowd uproars and horde brutality is the thing that lost all sense of direction in the outrage.

I think close to 100% about all individuals would concur that Black Lives Matter, I figure any normal individual would concur with this. Probably "bigot" President Donald Trump immediately showed up to openly endorse this idea after the killing of George Floyd, the individual whose passing on account of the police that was credited as supercharging the Black Lives Matter development (BLM) in 2020. I additionally consider close to 100% individuals would concur that police ought not shoot unarmed individuals that don't present a danger to life or to the public.

Despite these 2 basic ideas, the explanation of fixing these issues lost all sense of direction in the horde dissent and mobs. Presumably shrewd ideas like more and better police preparing that is commanded (most likely on a Federal Level), or blended policing with social laborers, or policing that stresses struggle de-acceleration may be savvy reaction or message that would come from protest.

nstead, the crowd needed to simply undermine the police. Dispose of the police all together.

The crowd would never see the value in the intricacy of policing, in that occasionally the police may defy equipped individuals holding their own families prisoner, or savage packs that would assume control over the city and kill unpredictably... ..or far more terrible, as perhaps police facing circumstances like having an exposed 6 foot 8 inch tall 350 pound buddy jumped up on some medication like PCP or Heroin holding a cleaver swinging at anything that moved shouting I'm a "Bare Ninja!"

Best of karma Mr. Social specialist, the police will simply remain back and let you handle this one.

No matter the significance of policing, or the sturdiness and intricacy of the work. People of color Matter! Undermine the police.

… Even however surveys at the time showed that more than 75-80% of the African-American people group needed to keep the police, and add more changes and root out the trouble makers that coincidentally had a badge.

No matter, this was a HOT POLITICAL issue, thinking be damned.

How did all this warped thinking come to be?

A couple of the extremely straightforward reasons there was such a lot of conflict in America in the 21st century is in reality very simple.

Much of it was political.

- The rich have ALWAYS wanted cheap labor, labor they could get cheap or export to cheap locations, this helped make them rich, whether it be exporting jobs to China or bringing in waves of Latin American immigrants, cheap labor keeps production costs low (and thus profit). The super rich in America have had so much power and influence over the last 30 years that BOTH Republicans and Democrats supported this concept of exporting jobs and allowing illegal immigrants. Because of the endless supply of laborers who will "do it for less than the other guy," wages for the middle class have gone DOWN for over 30 years. Because of the job destruction that accelerated in the 21st century, the middle class and lower class were increasingly diminished and broken on both the political right and left.

- Because the middle class has been crushed to a large degree through chronic unemployment and declining standard of living, Donald Trump was elected to turn these first two concepts on their heads and had done so with some level of success…and dissention.

The working class has consistently been an ESSENTIAL part of American satisfaction, as happenstance, and up, versatility, and solace, and the expectation for a superior life for themselves as well as their kids has been a HALLMARK of the American example of overcoming adversity. This as in addition to a couple could have the American dream, yet MILLIONS could have the American dream. Through work, training, exertion and drive, a superior life was conceivable. The working class life in America conveyed this better life for DECADES.

After the monetary accident of 2008, and abroad product of good American blue collar positions, this sort of life turned out to be progressively hard to attain.

- Another component of the reasons of the American strife of the

21st century is the incredible social elites in New York, Washington DC, Hollywood and San Francisco have consistently been beguiled by liberal philosophies and have transformed into a larger number of ideologues than brains. The dissidents and Democrats, regardless of legislative issues, will ALWAYS assault Republicans, Conservatives, and private enterprise, and people groups of all confidence regardless of the reason, regardless of the explanation. Presently dissidents are dumping on moderates and individuals in the middle.

When Trump and the working class were making advances after the appointment of 2016, the elites in government, media, and enormous business did what ever they could to obliterate Trump and the working class revolt. From farce denunciations, to counterfeit news, to counterfeit dossiers utilized as a guise to research for high "wrongdoings", the elites in government and the media retaliated against the working class revolt, as the working class revolt would crash the nonconformists or partnerships longs for wealth, or communism, or most POWER.

This working class revolt was VERY like the working class revolt that happened in the UK with their Brexit, as there the elites held off the partition with the EU for quite a long time and utilized each legitimate and social apparatus available to them too to hold the crush spirit from occurring. France (with their Yellow Vest development) and Italy additionally went through huge famous working class uprisings, as did Brazil and numerous different countries. For each situation, the rich needed to hold tight to their modest work, and nonconformists had dreams of one world government, or all out communism, and didn't have any desire to go down without a fight.

- The Democrats and the elites, in an effort to maintain their power and get rid of Trump and the middle-class revolt, had seen that their biggest, best, and most reliable voting base, African- Americans, were beginning to ask questions. Democrats have been in almost 100% control of minority and inner-city communities for DECADES, and in some places a century or more and the black lives had not really improved. As a result, the Democrats would do anything to keep the blacks on their side…including stoking the flames of a race war if necessary, by calling all those on the other side Nazi-Racist-Klan   members…

and these Klan individuals never call their moms either to beware of them… and I once saw one of them kick a dog.

… … whatever it took.

Create a mob and shock. Call the opposite side bigots. Keep your dark democratic square on your side.

- And lastly, of the American strife of the 21st century, as the liberals and Democrats had gravitated towards cultural-centric careers in – the media, academia, and entertainment (Hollywood)
  - had assumed control over the schools and our way of life and had for more than the last 30-40 years inculcated, simplified, and propagandized understudies in American schools for generally all that time. Ideas like social sensitivity and their aides were pushed and advanced. Free reasoning and non-congruity were squashed – ordinarily by the "shock" of different understudies. Subsequently, understudies were simplified and propagandized to so they can be controlled all the more without any problem. Understudies were not generally told "how" to think, however rather taught with regards to "what" to think.

This made armies of foolish uproar and dissent zombies or serious communists themselves. They couldn't have cared less with regards to working class esteems and portability, they were either excessively youthful and couldn't have cared less, or the framework didn't convey monetarily, and they had abandoned the system.

Because of this large number of elements that developed during the 21st century, a social conflict, a conflict that began in the 1960's, developed to arrive at minimum amount, and mass allure, by the mid 2000's, and was set by the appointment of Barack Obama in 2008 and 2012.

As President Obama couldn't convey salvation for the working class during his term in office, the working class retaliated in the appointment of 2016, and decided in favor of Trump, and the elites and the dug in "Underground government" in government revulsed in shock and frightfulness. In 2016, the working class had an amazing weapon in Donald Trump that battled the elites better than they at any point could expect or dream of. Thus, the left needed to retaliate against Donald Trump to keep up with quite a bit of their control and power.

Fight back with a fury.

hose retaliating, not just utilized political apparatuses like hoax examinations concerning Russian conspiracy or farce arraignment endeavors in Ukrainian impact selling they additionally utilized social devices like the media, the scholarly community, and Hollywood to keep up with their control, and they utilized America as a bludgeon, or an instrument to achieve their mission.

- "Traditional America is bad."
- "Traditional America is evil."
- "Traditional America is not as good as it was said to be."

This is on the grounds that Donald Trump had drawn first blood utilizing America as a club first with his mission trademark "Make America Great Again." subsequently, to counter the Trump account, the left needed to complement the negative, dispose of the positive, and at times modify American history.

or instance –

he nonconformists will say - The Pilgrims came to America to take land from Native Americans!

However, the dissidents will not say; The Pilgrims escaped strict narrow mindedness, savagery, and murder in Europe and were displaced people escaping with no genuine spot to go – Liberals will additionally say Central Americans are outcasts are meriting safe-haven and can take the positions of the working class… yet Pilgrims… no such tolerance.

Another Example may be -

merica has consistently been a bigoted country! They made and progressed slavery!

However, the nonconformists will not say; Slavery was seen by most Americans and an anathema and was prohibited in the North before the Constitution was even marked... subsequently making America. The main explanation the North didn't battle immediately was they didn't need the South to align with Britain to return and pulverize their revolution.

...Sometimes legislative issues makes monstrous bed fellows.

... This is without a doubt one of the misfortunes of the genuine world. Another Example may be -

he Republicans are bigoted and have consistently been racist!

owever, the dissidents and elites will not say; The Republicans were framed as a bondage abolitionist party. Abraham Lincoln, a Republican, liberated the slaves. Other present day occasions like, that Republicans entry of the Civil Rights demonstration of 1964, in spite of a greater part of Democrats casting a ballot against it, or that the Democrats were generally the segregationist Jim-Crow-law party, from the Reconstruction of the Civil War to Woodrow Wilson, to George Wallace. These realities are helpfully hidden away from plain view by Democrats and liberals.

People that realize history know the intricacies behind the genuinely charged trademarks of each political party.

Now to say the Republicans have done nothing off-base themselves is obviously false... .and to become tied up with the ludicrous affectedness of Democrats and nonconformists is likewise delusion.

This is essential for the political cycles of ALL nations in the world.

ome great, some terrible, this is definitely not an American issue... this is a human problem.

hese days America is tossed squarely in the center of these human contentions, issues... .and desires.

... and "America" pays the price.

Change the System, Change America!

An option in contrast to "America?"

We previously inquired as to whether America is awful, America is off-base, and America is awful?

Many, especially those on the extreme passed on absolutely need to lump it all together and toss all of America in the waste stack and begin once again with a spotless sheet of paper.

We realize that "America" is an assortment of individuals, bound together through laws and a constitution, customs, and culture, and those individuals are particularly liable for articulating what America is at that time.

As ALL things should be decided by their other option, assuming not America, what? Some will say "everything except America!"… Anything however this "system."

Well, this negative, as often as possible politicized outlook has been explained somewhat for quite a long time in schools, and in the media, and even some of the time by Hollywood.

What many don't understand is that this disdain of America and disdain of this "framework" is propagandized disdain… .and assuming they disdain America, what is the alternative?

ell, a lot of this "America disdain" is simply disdain by disdain filled Marxists, disdain filled communists, and disdain filled nonconformists, and disdain filled agitators, these gatherings are in reality bowed on exhaustively cutting America down… .not making America consistently better, or fixing America, yet obliterating America.

Since it's initiation, America has attempted to be the cheerful unspoiled spot every one of us imagines in our own heads. Nonetheless, nowadays, there is by all accounts excessively "corporatism", or "corporate greed" are surely a few angles that twist our bliss or now and again real factors, yet this isn't the main thing making

Americans unhappy.

America has battled about what our "way of life" ought to be, and of that which will satisfy every one of us. A great deal of times these notions regarding how to accomplish joy come from academia.

… Quite frequently they fail.

Those in scholarly community or other extreme left social positions may say, we aren't about disdain – we additionally have a message! Uniformity and Utopia!

This is certifiably not an American peculiarity alone. A bunch of convictions that many individuals all over the planet embrace is a confidence in "all out" uniformity. This pathway to Utopia or Nirvana would accept these equivalent or populist standards. This sounds great!

I think we as a whole concur we ought to have balance of chance, and of admittance to training, and of the equivalent capacity to vie for a job.

However, this is deluding - While we as a whole blessing fairness of chance, not every person favors correspondence of result, as nobody can at any point ensure or anticipate a result. To ensure and result for somebody would be the speediest method for getting them to plunk down on their butt… .and do the absolute minimum… on the off chance that anything at all.

- If we are all equal who gets the beach house?
- If we are all equal who gets the fun jobs and who has to do the dirty jobs?

Total uniformity, and "balance of result" has been attempted ordinarily, most eminently beginning with the compositions and lessons of Karl Marx from the 1800's.

arl Marx was a scholarly from Europe in the last part of the 1800's, who "speculated" a reality where everybody is something very similar and gets something very similar (This was typically refined by taking from the rich, yet the center class).

However, it wasn't Karl Marx calling for change in individuals' lives.

Dissidents DEMAND CHANGE!

Liberals, or should I say "American style nonconformists" are individuals that need nonstop change in the public eye (regardless of whether it be positive or negative. They without a doubt need change, since they are rarely glad and need individuals to adjust to their misery and their feelings.). A portion of these nonconformists are Anarchists (individuals that need to disintegrate all administration), and generally these dull and void spirits simply disdain everybody, normally none more so than themselves.

Now, in all honesty, some of the time these grumbling gatherings do have a point, there are indeed some terrible things that emerged from American history. Each individual on the planet and each country in history has had some terrible. This is the thing that makes us human, and standing up to these terrible things permits us some contemplation into getting it fixed.

However, hearing how America is just awful is absurd.

Today, when we talk about America that conversation is solely about its disappointments and weaknesses. This is on the grounds that nonconformists, Marxists, and communists in their visually impaired disdain of America have harmed the public exchange, and the traditional press continually hoping to communicate the preposterous to get evaluations, has established a climate where the aggregate story can seldom track down whatever great to say about America.

People that get truth, and embrace reason, and genuine grant, realize that OVERWHELMINGLY there is a whole lot, all the more great that emerged from America and American history than dissidents EVER need to admit.

Hearing a contrary history of America from individuals that think they have done nothing off-base themselves is delusion.

For instance, for quite a long time dissidents have lectured "resilience" and "love"... .but nowadays you see these equivalent individuals crushing up and consuming urban areas, restricting and obstructing moderate scholars and speakers via online media and on school campuses.

Where is the "affection", and where is the "resistance" liberals?

Not to say nonconformists have NEVER done anything great. Radicalism, and reformism, has had numerous triumphs, especially in the space of safeguarding social liberties. Nonconformists have had numerous social liberties triumphs, and they rest on

those shrubs, yet they additionally have had numerous social equality disappointments, or utilized their "social liberties" childishly to the mishap of others.

Some of these battles on occasion have extended the domain of "social equality", as the familiar saying had been your social equality end where my being starts. In this, a few "social equality" activities have been dangerous to others and even families.

Liberals have arrived at a point in their advancement where they need to examine the mirror, as they appear to carry out considerably more wrongdoing and violations against humankind than America itself could possibly do. From the dissidents embrace of medications, fetus removal, woke horde brutality, restriction, terrorizing and doxing of those they can't help contradicting; nonconformists, Marxists, revolutionaries, and communists clownishly and childishly appear to have their own disappointments, alongside advantageous recollections... .as they battle to contain their extremist inclinations and desire for power.

The nonconformists in media and the scholarly community just appear to specifically take a gander at the awful parts of human activities and fault it on a whole country... Nearly these events aren't really an American attribute alone, as ALL countries and ALL mankind wrestle with these issues.

spirational America, the genuine America, the America WE ALL WANT, the genuine America, the America we as a whole know and yearn for, is being distorted.

As these America critics would say America has welcomed awful things on the world, individuals that realize the realities realize that America liberated itself and the world from servitude, liberated the world from government, and Nazism, and death camps, and won the Cold War. America additionally made wondrous developments in science and medication that likewise saved millions… maybe billions of lives also. We don't hear this story much from these skeptics or from liberal scholarly world these days.

That is on the grounds that more elevated level the scholarly community in schools and colleges are broken, degenerate, and infected.

<u>MARXISM HAS NEVER LIVED UP TO ITS HYPE OR PROMISE</u>

Even however America won the Cold War against the Marxists and socialists in the Soviet Union, the contamination of socialism like a COVID-19, didn't disappear altogether, as it spread here to America and arrived in our colleges… .as these educators never lived in a Marxist nation and just know about the romanticized publicity regarding how incredible they socialism and Marxism is… .while millions kicked the bucket in "secret."

As Ronald Reagan once broadly said –

> *How would you tell a Communist?*
>
> *ell, it's somebody who understands Marx and*
>
> *Lenin. Also how would you tell an enemy of*
>
> *Communist?*
>
> *It's somebody who gets Marx and Lenin.*

In their agreeableness, these individuals in more elevated levels of the scholarly world need to trust the lies of Marxism, as individuals in more significant levels of the scholarly community will quite often be effectively controlled by passionate contentions that are not experimentally acceptable. In their intrinsic shortcoming, these more elevated level scholarly sorts are generally not of solid person. The scholarly world in their agreeableness and frail person has been ready contender for the spread of Marxist thoughts as they have been for right around a century.

It isn't simply in scholarly world that there is bending and individuals of feeble person, however in the media also. Individuals of feeble person in the media need to recount to a story that will sell the most papers. Mobs, annihilation and tumult will quite often sell a ton of papers. This is entirely typical as Communism and Marxism shows complaints, and outrage, and unrest, and isolates individuals into gatherings and sets one in opposition to one more to assume responsibility for a general public through revolution.

We see a lot of this upset start in sculpture crushing, and uproars, and torching… ..and the news gobbles this up as they sell broadcast appointment and more papers.

The explanation this isn't countered, is on the grounds that we are losing information on the

real factors of this present reality, or things like history, or that information on this present reality that is conveyed to us by a one-sided and degenerate the scholarly world of today, is poisoned.

Academia today is practically 90% liberal, as the nonconformists in colleges have removed moderate educators and voices. This way they can contort grant to "their method of thinking"

To obliterate information and twist insights, the Marxists need to delete history. 100 years prior the Marxists deleted history in Russia, they eradicated history in China, and in any remaining grounds the philosophy dominated. Presently the Marxists need to eradicate American history, and at last need to delete America. On the off chance that they can delete American memory, they can annihilate America. This is on the grounds that the best story and most awesome aspects of America are rousing and elevating. These accounts unite us as a people.

Because America is an elevating story and an industrialist nation, and private enterprise offers individuals trust and motivation, Marxists, communists, and nonconformists need to annihilate it. This is on the grounds that their contending philosophical framework is distorted and broken. While America offers trust and opportunity, Marxism, communism, and socialism just offers dis-motivator and intimidation to make their framework work… .and that is hopelessness, the direct inverse of America and its opportunity and its inspiring story and history.

ot to say we ought not at any point hear or defy the terrible. We ought to. This is truth and permits us to have a degree of reflection and can make enhancements to America.

For instance, in all honesty, the private enterprise we have in the West and in America separates now and again… like during the Great Depression. It additionally appears to have separated today, where we sent huge number of occupations to China in desires to construct an exchange with China and to build benefit. Sadly, we received minimal consequently other than a carport loaded with modest broken machines and lot of unemployment.

When free enterprise separates Marxism becomes elegant, particularly in these cases where there is financial disturbance. Monetary interruption should consistently be held in line in industrialist frameworks, as a solid economy makes a sound society. An undesirable economy creates

issues… .issues America's adversaries like Marxists rush to underwrite on.

Capitalism additionally separated in the 1930's during the Great Depression, and Marxism and socialism became famous in America… .briefly. Our American Grandparents and Great Grandparents were shrewd individuals, as they said we needn't bother with socialism, we without a doubt need to fix free enterprise, which they did. After they fixed it, America had the best quality of living on the planet for a really long time. This is elevating. In the mean time, socialism after the 1930's proceeded with torment, murder, seizure, wretchedness, and detainment on the size of millions in the USSR and China… .bummer fellows… .Communism absolutely sucks.

n a Marxist framework they put stock in taking from everybody and rearranging that abundance in a way they see fit. They become the masters, divine beings on the planet, and you should be submissive to THEM.

This is oppression and Marxists don't need you to know that.

he explanation Marxists in their upright daydream need to mutilate current realities and history, have no other strategy of getting individuals to their side other than pressure, so they conceal realities and history.

Since Marxists and communists can't actually spur individuals in their social orders, they HAVE to subjugate and kill to advance "their image" of social request and "their image" of "civil rights." The killing and annihilation and detainment of Marxism and socialism and extreme left communism exceeds all logical limitations and knows no end.

People should adjust in a Marxist or communist framework or they will be undermined, or detained, or tormented, or most noticeably terrible of all killed.

… however Marxists will not let you know that, they put on a beautiful face, and let you know how brilliant their general public is… .as they try to obliterate yours.

Don't accept it?

Look up the historical backdrop of spots where they attempted to force Marxism, socialism and extreme left communism. In places like the Soviet Union, or Communist China, or the Khymer Rouge in Cambodia… ..millions were

killed… .by the public authority… ..all in the "Expectations" of everybody being equivalent and having precisely the same thing.

Despite all the killing, not every person was made equivalent or had precisely the same thing… ..regardless of the multitude of endeavors… .notwithstanding all the killing.

ome would say, well they had types of communism in places like Sweden and Norway and in those nations it worked astoundingly. … .till it didn't. These nations that are homogeneous and everybody gets along, attempted enormous scope government communism, and it fizzled. Accordingly, they went to limited scope communism and made free enterprise the center of their economies and societies.

ruth be told, there are as of now a few types of limited scope communism pretty much all over (counting here in America), and in certain spots it works… to some degree (… and believe it or not I would even supporter for limited scope, and transitory social projects… on occasion). In any case, with enormous scope communism, in places like downtown America, it is a disaster.

Despite all the proof against huge scope communism and Marxism, the philosophy still so regularly focuses on "valuable simpletons" like Bernie Sanders (who I believe is a hero… yet is absolutely hallucinating and confused), assuming individuals like Bernie Sanders get power, the Marxists then, at that point, just need to assume responsibility for Bernie Sanders (which they as of now have done generally thoughtfully) to execute their agenda.

hat is intriguing in America today is that both Donald Trump and Bernie

Sanders recognize the truth about the economy... .broken. The distinction between the two is that Donald Trump has a solution to fix the economy that is very surprising than Bernie Sanders. Trump favors fixing private enterprise, a framework that empowers individual opportunity and permits people to make items and bring in cash. Bernie favors communism and needs to take from you what you make and give it to other people... .at THEIR discretion.

But you don't realize that Bernie needs to take from you, Bernie has a vibe decent message - Equality for everybody (that never turns out equivalent regardless of how much communism and Marxism attempts). To get you to accept their framework works, they lie. Furthermore the untruths must be conveyed to everybody, this is the reason assuming responsibility for culture is important.

To assume responsibility for a general public, the Marxists, extreme left communists, and dissidents need

to pursue the instruments of culture. The apparatuses of culture being the schools, the media, and the mainstream society diversion focuses... .in America this is Hollywood.

ecause if Marxists, and extreme left communists, and the dissidents can assume responsibility for the way of life, they can handle the mind.

If they can handle the brain, they can get POWER!

Power over you, control over your family, control over your method of life.

nfortunately, this takeover is as of now in progress, and they are coming to get you and your family. Check out the steadily expanding weird and controlling things schools need you to do today. Wasn't their unique mission to show perusing, composing, and number juggling? Presently they are showing things like how to be a civil rights champion and change the world.

Change it to what? Communism? Political agitation? Extreme left socialism?

Thanks, I'll pass. Since I know reality and I know history, and I and the Founding Fathers know human nature.

However, in light of the fact that this takeover by the extreme left is as of now in progress, we want to stop this.

We can stop this with the truth.

It all starts with history... .A background marked by us all... .A background marked by battle... .A past filled with what works.

Join us as we recount the best story ever told,

... .The historical backdrop of America

A GREATNESS BORN
OF STRUGGLE

U- - S- - A!!...U- - S- - A!!!....U- - S- - A!!!...U- - S- - A!!!

- The blasting and loud serenade emitting from the group at the 1980 Lake Placid Olympics, as the titanic longshot, U.S. Olympic Hockey Team, retaliated to score on the USSR and tied the game 3-3.

... in a game America would at last win.

America is a country of heroes.

Do you think just ONE gathering in America needed to struggle?

... .please

he account of American is about battle... the tale of battle is the tale of the human condition. You need to attempt to improve life NO MATTER THE IDEOLOGY, regardless of whether it be private enterprise or communism or Marxism.

Marxism, communism, and extreme left radicalism certainly gives us battle, yet seldom conveys achievement, satisfaction, and success... just stories of how things will be extraordinary, just to be trailed by wretchedness for everyone.

To Far-left nonconformists and Marxists, in the present "populist," everything is equivalent babble universe of overt sensitivity, America is no more excellent than some other nation, similar to say Luxembourg. As though Luxembourg won two World Wars and strolled on the moon. No, sorry Politically Correct, disdain filled crying populist nonconformists… .not every person gets a prize, not all things are not equivalent, America isn't care for different nations on the planet, everything isn't awful with America. America was better before it lost a lot of its way throughout the most recent 20 years because of political correctness.

Is America great? No (… .yet give us time). America certain as damnation will not be made better or have "progress" by outrage, annihilation, division, and detestation. It sure will not be improved by misery or savagery. It will not be improved by subjugating Americans to unpayable obligation or totalitarianism.

America should attempt to continue to improve. Fortunately, today we have a framework.

WAS AMERICA EVER GREAT?

Today, American nationalism is undesirable. Those that call themselves nationalists are regularly ridiculed, put down, and at times chuckled at, as most conventional convictions and qualities are chronologically erroneous or overhauled in a negative manner by liberal storytellers.

nyone that says America was never extraordinary is a self-loathing, discouraged, indoctrinated, grumbler needing mental assessment. They have been deceived by an inexorably liberal scholarly community, self-despising and tight in their updated introspection.

We definitely realize that with private enterprise that conquering the negative parts of the human condition is the American significance. America makes opportunity, longer lives, riches, and a pathway to self governance.

oday, few transparently battle for America. Regularly this is on the grounds that they are debilitated by those negative, morose, crying and crying nonconformists that have assumed control over universities and the scholarly world, or assumed control over the bad culture of traditional press, or by the dissidents that have dominated and tracked down asylum in the joys and dream and evil in Hollywood; All of these foundations consolidated to capture or co-pick the social account of America, and of America's greatness.

Well, fortunately, the majority of us know unique. We know the genuine story of the incredible country that is the United States of America. Numerous normal sensible individuals realize that dissidents will more often than not portray the extraordinary country of America, as they simply take the parts that were without a doubt terrible and detonate those awful occasions like it were OUR ENTIRE history.

The genuine story of America is that America was based on battle and difficulty, and through the finesse of God, those people of America did prevail after their battle and now and again rose to significance; this, to brilliantly make a superior world their kids, for our kids, and for the world at large, which America has saved over and over.

America had made a framework that permitted more than some other country on the planet, people to accomplish significance through difficult work, exertion, and some penance and struggle.

Martin Luther King will be associated with hundreds of years if not longer due to the battle he needed to persevere. The best of his thoughts, thinking, and will suffer in view of his battle to achieve the correct thing. Besides you could put incredible Americans like Arthur Ashe, Frederick Douglass, and Harriet Tubman into this equivalent class too… .and indeed, a case for Colin Kaepernick could be made for this also (however I disagree with his methodology).

America isn't better for those that attempted to accomplish the WRONG thing like Julius and Ethel Rosenbeg, who parted with US Atomic privileged insights to the Soviets, or rebels that have utilized savagery as their instrument to accomplish the obliteration of the awful pieces of America, yet the great too. For reasons unknown there are some in scholarly community that appear to celebrate this.

America's achievement in the past was not only because of its initial guidelines and chiefs, however it obligation to the free-endeavor framework. This permitted INDIVIDUALS to prosper, this is one motivation behind why America had turned into a country of heroes.

Guiding American directors permitted the Wright Brothers the drive and motivation to foster controlled trip before the remainder of the world. They had numerous preliminaries and blunders, however in the long run succeeded.

Speaking of experimentation, directing American directors helped push Thomas Edison in the 1800's to imagine world changing items like the light, film camera, and phonograph to record sound. He additionally further developed existing items like the message and phone and had a larger number of licenses and creations than any American ever.

American significance and directing administrators helped fuel industry and permitted business titans like John Rockefeller to change the oil business to fuel our development, Henry Ford to alter the vehicle business, Andrew Carnegie to upset the Steel business, and Steve Jobs to reform the PC and individual gadget industry. There are large number of Americans in business and industry that have improved the world. To name them all, and detail every one of their achievements, this book would need to be more than 1,000,000 pages long.

Leaders that changed the world and IMPROVED a large part of the human

condition.

merican significance and directing directors permitted Charles Lindbergh fly solo across the Atlantic to demonstrate it very well may be done when so many before him had fizzled. Permitted ladies like Amelia Earhart a brief time later, to accomplish similar achievement as Lindbergh to demonstrate ladies through expertise and fortitude could do it as well.

truth be told, American ladies have accomplished more than some other ladies all through the world. Counting bringing up their own youngsters to be the GREAT makers and achievers. In a country of extraordinary achievers and incredible achievements, for what reason do as such numerous effective individuals thank their moms first? American moms should have something going on that aided make this country great.

It appeared on occasion that American ladies that played their parts decreased as their male partners appeared to get the most reputation. Notwithstanding, as Fred Astaire's most incessant dance accomplice Ginger

Rogers would show, she could do EVERYTHING Fred Astaire did, just in reverse and in high heels.

As for Hollywood ladies that added to the accomplishment of America, endless celebrities elected to engage the soldiers to support their confidence and spirits, and one Hollywood Star, the delightful and splendid Hedy Lamarr, thought carefully in a conflict work to assist with further developing weapons like torpedoes, and unstable vicinity wires on arms (Nowadays, it seems like Hollywood stars simply torpedo America). So persuasive were Hedy Lamarr's thoughts and creations, that a portion of her ideas from more than 50 years prior gave a structure to present day gadgets like Bluetooth, Wi-Fi, and GPS.

It isn't simply individual people that have accomplished significance in America, however individual gatherings that have had extraordinary achievement, those that have gotten tied up with America. This, as in proof of Asian and Hispanic Americans, are a lot richer and more fruitful here in America than they would have been had they remained in their home countries.

In the American mixture we tried to acquire the most awesome aspects of different networks and societies and consolidate them to our own, in any event, for individuals who were at that point here. One could contend that the Environmental Movement that came to fruition and power here in America, that will keep the earth clean for our

people in the future, was to a great extent because of the local American otherworldliness and association with the land and earth... .and the world will be better for this thinking.

The distinction among America and different countries of the world is that America has frequently transcended the terrible pieces of human instinct through law, instruction, customs and culture, difficult work and battle. In this structure, with our industrialist framework, America additionally made astonishing accomplishments, accomplishments no other country on the planet or in mankind's set of experiences can match.

The American banner on the moon is confirmation of that.

America epitomizes the human soul of experience, disclosure, and achievement.

…..IN THE BEGINNING

Far-left Liberals, Marxists, Socialists, and Anarchists that populate the scholarly community disdain Columbus, and they need to consider him responsible for his "violations"… .and nail it to all of America.

Well, Columbus was not an American, he didn't live under American laws, yet I will respond to the call of contrasting Columbus with the present dissidents, and how he isn't any more regrettable than they are, and indeed Columbus may be a preferred individual over they are.

We all realize that Columbus found the New World in 1492, a few hundred years after Leif Ericson, and indeed, there were at that point Native individuals living here as of now for millennia. Columbus is given unfavorable criticism by nonconformists as Columbus didn't set out from Spain hoping to take, or colonize, or bring slaves, or kill individuals, as Columbus in his first journey was searching for a course toward the east to build up exchange routes.

Liberals with their "amazing world" speculations and negative thoughts of all that is Western Civilization and their optimism about uninformed "honorable savages," disdain Columbus.

Liberals appear to mix around the account of the apparently serene Arawoks whom Columbus "persecuted." Liberals of today will more often than not disregard a portion of different clans Columbus experienced like the Cigüayos, who were a warlike clan that attempted to assault the campaign, or the inhuman Carib Indians of St. Croix that likewise started assaults on Columbus' endeavor (possibly irritated him)... . There isn't quite a bit of discuss these clans or "honorable savages" from nonconformists of today, whom Columbus was simply hoping to exchange with.

Perhaps Columbus most noteworthy sin is that he acquainted Christianity with the New World, and we as a whole realize that dissidents of today disdain Jesus with a passion.

As referenced, Columbus was not an American. However he had a few characteristics that America would embrace and accept a few attributes America would disavow. No one is great. Columbus was likely not a holy person as he or individuals from his endeavor did ultimately kill and detain individuals, regularly to safeguard themselves, as in reality there are not many holy people.

History is constantly decided through various crystals of time and culture. Would you be able to envision assuming Columbus arrived in America today? Columbus could say he arrived in a universe of massive savages. He would check out a portion of individuals here and presumably attempt to socialize and Christianize those that arrangement drugs, take part in uproars, fire related crime, and annihilating others' shops and businesses

for the sake of "Civil rights." Columbus may likewise see the sex dealing, the medication use and the shootings and viciousness in downtown, and think America is however malevolent as it seems to be deceptive of him.

Furthermore, Columbus may attempt to acquaint the idea of marriage with those making a lot of children and appallingly forsaking them. Columbus could reverse the situation and compose a background marked by nonconformists. Columbus could compose of the dissidents about their annihilation of the Americas as rough, drug ingesting, irate, atheist and flippant individuals, however as we realize that would just be a little piece of the genuine in general story of the present America.

Columbus in his investigation faced tremendous individual and expert challenge and enduring, all in the quest for shipping lanes to experience the main "American Dream." His excursion to America and into the obscure was intrinsically risky and he could have kicked the bucket numerous times.

n this present reality, (a world wherein nonconformists don't appear to possess), Columbus' greatest commitment to history is that his investigations carried a road to cautioning Europe, the predominant culture of capacity and edification of that period, to the presence of America. In his revelation, success, colonization, and Christianization followed, yet in addition as well, another renaissance of human investigation, advancement, and disclosure detonated and changed the world perpetually; once in a while for the more awful, most regularly for the improvement of further developing the human condition.

For nonconformists that overturn Columbus sculptures as a rule their greatest accomplishment in life is getting the high score in the area on HALO or their beloved video game.

… ..Now that we have uncovered liberal fantasies, bends, fancies, and their idiocies, back to a genuine history of America's significance; as told through the crystal of that which changed the world significantly and ordinarily to improve things, as history of the world through a liberal "exploitation account" is uncovered, exposed, and thoroughly bitch slapped.

OF OUR FOREFATHERS

Within a time of Columbus' first undertaking, wayfarers went to the new world from France, Britain, Holland, Spain and Portugal. They investigated the new world and exchanged with Indians and took the new universes wealth back home. It required 100 years after Columbus for the principal effective endeavors to settle America from England to happen; the Virginia state in 1607 and the Pilgrims at Plymouth in the Massachusetts province in 1620.

hen the Pilgrims arrived here, there were at that point European individuals here, for quite a long time. A settlement in Florida and out of every other place on earth Santa Fe New Mexico in the focal point of North America, a long way from any port. These current Spanish states didn't shape the predominant culture of the country that was to become America that pushed it ahead with power, coming full circle on the world stage the way and to the degree the Virginia and Massachusetts provinces did.

Settling the new world was incredibly, troublesome as the principal English settlement endeavor at Roanoke in 1587 totally vanished, and no hint of the pioneers was at any point found. It was not for years and years that the following arrangement of pilgrims in Plymouth and Virginia states had set out, and experienced comparative battles, as death paces of practically half inside the initial 2 years were seen. Without the assistance of the current Native Americans, the pioneers unquestionably would have vanished like those early pilgrims in Virginia at Roanoke. Without the Native American commitment definitely in this case, this nation would not have been molded the way it was.

simultaneously, individuals were settling America to get away from strict oppression, they were additionally other "travelers" escaping to different spots on the planet. These different explorers escaped to places wealthy in regular assets like South Africa, and South and Central America. Some way or another however, these regions didn't create in the ways like America did. They never became world powers and a prevailing power in human development.

So why America?

Maybe like grapes on the plant that need to "battle in their turn of events" to deliver a truly fine wine, America did as well, and America is unto itself like fine wine, may have been exceptional for that battle. More than

likely, the Founders and powerhouses welcomed better thoughts on administration dependent on this struggle.

As the battle to at first foster America was a constant fight with vulnerability, I don't know the number of individuals today would take up an undertaking where there is a 50/50 shot at death, and assuming they didn't kick the bucket, they were compensated with that vulnerability, close to starvation, and scarcely getting by.

t didn't seem like much fun.

I think numerous about individuals today that carry on with an existence of solace would decide to remain in the old world, give up to the battle, surrender their religion, and bear their hopeless destiny till death. For they are the kind of individuals that picked the simple way, those that would prefer to carry on with a dismal life on their knees asking and in subjugation, as opposed to dieing on their feet battling… .like the new Americans.

merica, since its initiation, saw its greatness in its struggles.

William Bradford was one of the first Pilgrim pioneers in the New World and filled in as Governor of the Plymouth Colony on and off for around 30 years somewhere in the range of 1621 and 1657. During his residency as Governor Bradford kept a diary that kept a point by point progress of the province and portrayed a portion of the difficulties that the Pilgrims persevered. Incredibly, his composing gives an extraordinary account of their battles as well as apparently showed what molded an exhaustive outline of the early American person. In his diary, he would compose

> *"Generally extraordinary and fair activities are went with incredible troubles, and both should be enterprised and overwhelmed with responsible courage."*

In one more section in his diary, William Bradford would remark on Gods Providence displayed towards the Pilgrims and this new settlement, and the country that should have been, and of it individuals that would follow, the American public. William Bradford would compose –

> *"Subsequently, out of little beginnings more prominent things have been created by His hand that made everything of nothing, and gives being to everything that are; and, as one little flame might light 1,000, so the*

> *light here ignited hath sparkled unto many..."*

In William Bradford's residency as lead representative, the state developed, and more youngsters were conceived, different pilgrims came from Europe, and as the settlement appeared to arrive at minimum amount, and seemed it would get by, and thrive, and would be a suitable substance going ahead, Bradford would later compose –

> *"May not and should not the offspring of these dads properly say: "Our dads were Englishmen which came over this incredible sea, and were prepared to die in this wild however they cried unto the*

Lord, and He heard their voice, and looked on their misfortune... . Allow them subsequently to applaud the Lord, since He is great, and His leniencies suffer for eternity. Yea, let them which have been reclaimed of the Lord, shew how He hath conveyed them from the hand of the oppressor. At the point when they meandered in the; desert wild far removed, and tracked down no city to stay in, both hungry, and parched, their spirit was overpowered in them. Allow them to admit before the Lord His caring benevolence, and His superb works before the children of men."

It was of men like William Bradford that lopsidedly formed the American person and inheritance, one that was to fill in worldwide height and suffer for many years… notwithstanding millennia.

Not simply the Pilgrims up north, yet early America's establishment likewise created in Virginia. The Virginia states likewise went through comparative battles and difficulties. Pioneers, for example, John Smith pushed that state through with difficult work, battle, penance, and help from the Native Americans to make their new province work.

John Smith would say in his diary;

Win or lose you won't ever lament buckling down, making penances, being focused or centering excessively. Achievement is estimated by what we have done to get ready for competition.

ohn Smith and William Bradford were pioneers and men of premonition and were energetic about what they had made. As a progression of different pioneers and pioneers came to America and worked and battled to make the new states work, another world unmistakable and unique in relation to the old world began to arise. Because of the seed and endeavors of these settlements, America's

character was molded, as America was to turn into a country that exemplified various qualities and unexpected thoughts in comparison to those that they were devoured by back in Europe. In their vision, in their work, in their plan, they would make another country considered in –

- Religious freedom and tolerance
- A practice of appreciation, and gratefulness to Gods providence
- Hard work, battle, and penance at times

•   Freedom and Political autonomyAnd DEMOCRACY! seed had been planted, and an establishment had been laid, a country was conceived whose relatives would ultimately proceed to save the world… .many occasions over. America would be a country, yet a signal on a slope and a focusing light to all, as the one little flame lit a by our predecessors hath for sure sparkled unto many… all through time and over numerous generations.

his new place that is known for America didn't go unrecognized in Europe, as others there longed for getting away from strict conflicts and had any desires for a superior life in another world. John Winthrop was an English priest that drove a gathering looking to track down escape from strict mistreatment, and he and a portion of his supporters concluded America may be that spot. In 1630 Winthrop gave a message to his assemblage in Southampton England to a considerable lot of those leaving with him on his experience to the new world. While getting ready to leave he realized that he had a mission, that was unmistakable from Europe and the Old World, and that mission would rise above that which preceded them.

In words reverberated by numerous Presidents since, including John Kennedy, Ronald Reagan, and Barack Obama, each would allude to John Winthrop's unique thought of this endeavor they set upon as filling in as a city upon a hill.

ohn Winthrop would say –

> *"For we should Consider that we will be as a City upon a Hill, the eyes surprisingly have arrived; so that in case we will manage our god in this work we have embraced thus cause him to pull out his current assistance from us, we will be made a story and an aphorism through the world, we will open the mouths of foes to talk evil of the methods of god and all educators for Gods purpose; we*

> *will disgrace the essences of large numbers of divine beings commendable workers, and cause their petitions to be transformed into Curses upon us till we be devoured out of the great land whether we are going: And to quiet down this talk with that admonishment of Moses that devoted worker of the Lord in his last goodbye to Israel (Deut. 30.) Beloved there is currently set before us life, and great, demise and evil in that we are Commanded this day to adore the Lord our God, and to cherish each other to stroll in his ways and to keep his Commandments and his Ordinance, and his laws, and the Articles of our Covenant with him that we might live and be*

increased, and that the Lord our God might favor us in the land whether we go to have it: But in case our hearts will dismiss so we won't comply, yet will be lured and love different Gods our joys, and benefits, and serve them, it is propounded unto us this day, we will without a doubt die out of the great Land whether we disregard this immense Sea to have it."

his feeling of mission and reason would fuel this assembly as they set out on an extraordinary endeavor, however a world transforming one also. America would be the new place where there is trust and promise.

AMERICAS INDEPENDENCE AND INTELLECTUAL GREATNESS WOULD GROW

As the Virginia and Massachusetts states had turned into a set up apparatus, America began to stretch out and furthermore retain an ever increasing number of pilgrims from the old world to the new world, and this developed the person that was at that point molded in America and directed its predetermination. As the 1600s advanced, America developed rapidly, by 1650 there were an expected 50,000 pilgrims in America, by 1700 a quarter million, by 1750 more than 1 million individuals called America home. As the primary pilgrims were tricked by a promising circumstance, others were moved by the strict mistreatments of a landmass in strict conflicts and political disturbance welcomed on by the Protestant Reformation. America became a position of chance, yet a safe space as settlers looked for freedom from the Old World.

s wars and strict disturbance cleared Europe, America saw what was occurring from a good ways, and was making a nation and arrangement of administration that would make preparations for those ills running over the Atlantic.

Nonetheless, however a different American character was creating, Europe and America were interlinked in terms of professional career and still by abroad principle, as the public conflicts among England and France poured out over to the provinces. Britain immediately united power and turned into the always nosy abroad expert of the colonies.

To pay for these costly conflicts, England needed to severely burden the states to help pay for it, regularly with little respect to the settlers' sentiments about the matter or a say how they were administered. These powers put all on an impact course; something began to fill in America, a progressive and free spirit.

As England inclined up tax collection and control of the American provinces, there was pushback to that tax assessment. This tax collection may be similar to how obligation is being heaped upon the youthful of today, who have no vote in its creation and advantage little from it. Shockingly today, there has been no genuine dissent of generational robbery, an issue apparently comparable to critical a dangerous atmospheric devation conjectures, yet some way or another silence.

This is the distinction of our precursors and ancestors, is that they had a stake in the game, and the accomplishment of their endeavors and thriving were reliant upon whether or not there was a devastating taxation rate and what sort of rule they lived under. (The present youthful appear to be more distractible by media and computer games and enthusiastic contentions and are less liberated from thought and are constrained by a King George identical philosophy in overt sensitivity... .it will be fascinating to perceive how long this all lasts.)

The surprising thing about our progenitors was their understanding into human instinct. However types of government have changed commonly in 5,000 years, Human nature has not. At the point when we take a gander at other new countries shaping in different nations, we now and then see strongmen that make new countries in their picture and outlook... that breakdown when they are killed by individuals they rule or they lose power... .typically the former.

Some different nations in our advanced world that make new countries and new administration that are desire and charming sounding don't endure much either, as they don't represent individuals they really oversee, but instead the sort of individuals they might want to administer... .this is right out of Ivory Tower

academia.

his is the thing that made our Founding Fathers unique.

Our Founding Fathers were savvy, all around educated, and they comprehended human instinct. They realized people jumped at the chance to be sluggish and needed things from the public authority and the public authority to deal with them. On the opposite side of the situation, they likewise realized an administration enjoyed outright ability to manage over its subjects, and left unchecked this standard would decay into tyranny.

This is the thing that made America extraordinary. American progressives, educated in the Age of Enlightenment perceived the truth about things, and could foster an agreement of how we should lead ourselves.

Patrick Henry would say to energizing cheers -

> *"Is life so dear, or harmony so sweet, as to be bought at the cost of chains and servitude? Restrict it, Almighty God! I know not what course others might take, but rather concerning me, give me freedom or give me death!"*

Messages like these observed a home in America as its progenitors were extraordinary journalists and speakers. In his leaflet "Presence of mind" Thomas Paine in 1776 would say-

> *"Opportunity hath been pursued round the globe. Asia and Africa have since a long time ago removed her. Europe respects her like an outsider, and England hath given her admonition to withdraw. O! Get the outlaw and plan in time a haven for mankind."*

It was voices like this that aided flash a transformation. Nonetheless, for America to be fruitful we would require great individuals and residents. In the hour of our Founding Fathers there was an extraordinary adherence to religion to make the best choice, for John Addams knew -

> *"We have no administration outfitted with power equipped for battling with human interests unbridled by ethical quality and religion... Our Constitution was made distinctly for a moral and strict individuals. It is completely lacking to the public authority of any other."*

This harmony between the public authority and its kin would ceaselessly run its course. Since individuals are essentially lethargic, and we have seen over the last a very long while that socialism has extraordinary charm in light of every one of its guarantees of cash to all. Nonetheless, in socialist framework the public authority takes from all, and provides for whom it picks. In a Democracy exactly the same thing can occur assuming we are not cautious with how we spend from the Treasury as Founding Father Ben Franklin knew-

> *When individuals observe that they can cast a ballot themselves cash, that will proclaim the finish of the republic."*

How might that finish of the Republic come? Communists have an approach, that they executed in numerous nations that exploits monetary, political, and social destabilization. Principal architects like James Madison, Benjamin Franklin, and Thomas Jefferson apparently realized how a nation could be undermined strategically and would attempt to place shields in our countries establishing documents.

It was important historic documents like the Declaration of Independence and Constitution that helped propel America to greatness.

The Declaration of Independence made this country. The Constitution characterized it. The Constitution characterized the construction of our administration, and the extremely significant Bill of Rights in that Constitution, is seemingly the main report on the planet, as it secured American Individuals privileges and freedoms.

his Bill of Rights held the public authority back from squashing the person. As it was people's endeavors and drive that prompted achievement, as such countless different states on the planet had neglected to realize.

Other Founding Fathers like Thomas Jefferson that knew whether an administration isn't receptive to its kin and attempts to run over them and enslave them and their freedoms they would be met by revolt. Jefferson would say-

> *"What nation can safeguard its freedoms in case its rulers are not cautioned now and again that their kin save the soul of opposition? Allow them to take arms."*

In all, the Founding Fathers were the ones who lectured opportunity, endeavor, work, and restraint. In our most prominent and most loved thought, freedom,

Thomas Paine in an open letter to the People of France said in 1792-

It is difficult to vanquish still up in the air to be free!"

As you could see, our progenitors were lively, and looked for individual opportunities found no place else on the planet.

Tax imposition without any political benefit was an issue that drove the Founding Fathers. By 1775, the disobedience and Revolution truly got moving as they could at this point don't bear English standard and order. In 1776 a Declaration of Independence was marked, and another country was authoritatively pronounced. Yet, England would not release them easily, America would need to battle a Revolutionary War for its opportunity and independence.

The settlers had some early triumphs and took trust in these little engagement triumphs, however at that point the full weight of British Imperial power, the most impressive power on the planet around then, re-upheld the armed forces currently here and hoped to squash all dissent.

George Washington was named by the Continental Congress to shape a military to battle, and that he did... or if nothing else attempted, as George Washington and the Americans were constantly beaten, steered, and almost totally obliterated on a few occasions.

It was in the difficulty in George Washington's breaking point, with a ceaselessly contracting armed force, at his colder time of year retreat at Valley Forge, Pennsylvania, that Washington's soldiers met extraordinary difficulty. They were under dressed and chilly, deprived and were close to starving. Notwithstanding, they would pull together and go ahead regardless of the cold, in spite of the absence of food and apparel, regardless of the difficulties, in spite of all chances. Battle on they did.

It wasn't only the military that suffered difficulty. As the underwriters of the constitution discovered, they essentially annoyed King George and the British Empire and felt their wrath. Every underwriter was a criminal that on occasion really needed to take off and escape for their lives, as many had property seized and burned.

As difficult stretches don't keep going as long as extreme individuals do, in his most obscure hours, George Washington got everyone excited and did the most insane thing. He assaulted. The Americans revitalized to battle the British at Trenton and won a

tremendous fight with little battle. Then, at that point, America following a couple of years they would begin to win a couple of different encounters, then, at that point, a couple of fights, then, at that point, a conflict itself. Eventually, America won in its conflict of freedom. On account of hard endeavors, thinking, and a longing to be free, as a free group can never be conquered.

THE INDUSTRIAL REVOLUTION AND AMERICA

Freed from the obligations of unfamiliar guideline, America was making excellent progress so far, correct with regards to the time the Industrial Revolution got moving, of which America was to turn into a colossal contributor.

American designers after the Revolution made the Cotton Gin, the main Suspension Bridge, Circular Saw and Milling Machine, Sewing Machine, Steam Ship, Combine Harvester, Steam Shovel, Telegraph and Morse Code, Rotary Printing Press, and the Jackhammer. All devices that would be effectively utilized to construct a country. The significance of the American Heritage happened from difficult work, penance, and accomplishing significance, and not on gifts or giveaways.

Americans fostered a person of difficult work, revelation, venture, advancement, and this prompted achievement and a superior method of life.

As America was rapidly turning into a world innovator in creation and mechanical turn of events, it didn't come quick enough, and notwithstanding this multitude of new devices, a few positions actually must be finished manually. A portion of this work that must be done, exploited free work as that was the best way to comprehend the work. As we probably are aware nothing is free, particularly if that "free" work will be work done by slaves, and most Americans of this period didn't care for or need subjection that was brought by the English beginning as ahead of schedule as 1619, as it ran incongruent to their convictions and better angels.

America was again running on one more impact course, this time it needed to stand up to its most exceedingly awful quality, bondage. Before the Revolutionary War even finished, and before there even was a national government, a few states began to boycott subjugation. Vermont prohibited subjection in 1777 and the greater part of New England took action accordingly before the established show was assembled. Yet, not all needed a finish to subjection, as states in the south stood up to… .and they opposed for decades.

AMERICA FIGHTS TO END SLAVERY

Some today may ask, for what reason didn't they pass a law-production bondage unlawful or forgo an enchanted wand and make everything disappear, thinking back to the 1800's?

It would be great of life were that simple and getting others to make the best decision were just basic. Individuals with personal stakes consistently stand up to. Certain individuals a long time from now may ask how individuals in the 21st century permitted late term early terminations not long before birth, and that those individuals advancing it were savage barbarians.

a similar inquiry may be posed of servitude over a century ago.

Through the 1840's and 1850's the degree of strain and dissent, and brutality encompassing the issue of subjection in America developed. In a political race far more petulant than Trump versus Clinton in 2016, the 1860 political race set off a firestorm, of dissent and severance. Before Lincoln was even introduced, states attempted to withdraw from the Union. As Lincoln got down to business, he would need to some way or another piece together the now dis-United States.

The underlying fights turned out poorly for the Union, and Lincoln was on occasion convinced by different lawmakers and consultants to think about a pathway for really dividing the United States in two, however Lincoln was having none of it.

AMERICA, AN IDEA WORTH FIGHTING FOR

Four score and seven years before the Battle of Gettysburg, our dads delivered, upon this mainland, another country, imagined in freedom, and committed to the recommendation that all men are made equivalent. Abraham Lincoln would proceed to say-

> *Now we are occupied with an incredible common conflict, testing whether that country or any country so considered thus committed, can long persevere. We are met on an extraordinary combat zone of that conflict. We have come to commit a part of that field, as a last resting place for the people who here gave their day to day routines that that country may experience. It is out and out fitting and legitimate that we ought to do this.*

> *But, from a bigger perspective, we can not devote - - we can not bless – we can not bless - - this ground. The bold men, living and dead, who battled here, have blessed it, far over our helpless ability to add or reduce. The world will little note, nor long recollect what we say here, however it can always remember what they did here. It is for us the living, rather, to be devoted here to the incomplete work which they who battled here have so far so respectably progressed. It is somewhat for us to be here committed to the extraordinary undertaking staying before us - - that from these regarded dead we take expanded dedication to that reason for which they gave the last full proportion of dedication - - that we here profoundly resolve that these dead will not have passed on to no end - - that this country, under God, will have another birth of opportunity - - and that administration of individuals, by individuals, for individuals, will not die from the earth.*

One thing that was not deniable is that this Civil War would have been battled, individuals will keep on being killed if vital, and President Abraham Lincoln would own it to the end.

America would have been one country, under God, inseparable, and without slavery.

Though America and the Union saw triumph at the clash of Gettysburg, that war didn't come without extra expense. More battling followed; more lives were lost.

In an original snapshot of beauty, Abraham Lincoln would be constrained to by and by address letters to certain families that lost friends and family in the battle for opportunity. One of them was the Bixby Letter, a concise letter of comfort sent in November 1864 to Lydia Parker Bixby, a widow living in Boston, who supposedly lost five children in the battle with the Union side. This well known letter also was one of Steven Speilberg's most noteworthy realistic accounts in narrating, as cited in the film Saving Private Ryan-

Executive Mansion,

Washington, Nov. 21, 1864.

Dear Madam,

I have been displayed in the records of the War Department an assertion of the Adjutant General of Massachusetts that you are the mother of five children who have kicked the bucket brilliantly on the field of battle.

I feel how powerless and unproductive should be any expressions of mine which should endeavor to bewilder you from the sadness of a misfortune so overpowering. However, I can't forgo offering to you the comfort that might be found in the thanks of the Republic they passed on to save.

ask that our Heavenly Father might soothe the pain of your mourning and leave you just the esteemed memory of the adored and lost, and the grave pride that should be yours to have laid so exorbitant a penance upon the special raised area of Freedom.

ours, truly and respectfully,

A. Lincoln.

This battle, and this penance would turn into a focal part of the American custom, as John Kennedy would say 100 years later.

"Let the word go forward from this overall setting to companion and adversary the same, that the light has been passed to another age of Americans—conceived in this century, tempered by war, restrained by a hard and harsh harmony, pleased with our antiquated legacy ... Let each country know, regardless of whether it hopes everything

America, and the best that is America, represents opportunity, retaliates against insidiousness, tyranny, and impractical notions that are oppressing and ruinous. Regardless of whether it be Taxation without portrayal during the 1700s, bondage during the 1800s, Imperial Japan, Nazism, Communism in the 1900's, or Islamofascisim, and Globalist Political Correctness of the 2000's, awesome of America will keep on facing oppression, impractical notions that subjugate, and false off track belief systems that look to destroy.

Today's "civil rights champions" unfortunately think all that they do puts them side of good (some of what they do is great, and a portion of their actions

are shockingly unnerving). Their reasoning is the same than ranch proprietors suspected they were in favor of good, or as socialists suspected they were. However they ensured the world they knew and felt OK with, all unfortunately didn't have a clue, or neglected, how huge parts of their belief systems ruined, subjugated, and destroyed the texture of what genuinely made a general public both practical and good.

What if individuals a long time from now liken early termination the same way individuals currently see servitude? Or on the other hand in case they see drug use, a medication utilize that made the narco-wars and murders in Latin America as the best unconfronted evil on the planet ever?

Social Justice Warriors think they are the beginning of progress to a superior way, a superior world... ..without understanding, NO, they were the OUTCOME of DECADES of extreme left belief system and conditioning, and they are the subsequent fizzled state.

When these "Civil rights Warriors" in 2020 attempted to assume responsibility for their daily routines and region they experienced in places like Seattle and Portland, they took in a hard illustration. Their ideal world" ran into a detour when some came to realize,

- They wanted a world without consequences and got out-of-control drug use.
- When they had out of control drug use getting things like food and medicine and order turned out to be challenging, they created chaos.
- They wanted a world without violence, and instead created a

world of chaos.

- When they tried to organize their world of chaos and bring order…they got a world of violence.

After many attacks, murders, assaults, and passings, individuals that generally lived in the space of occupation that didn't really have the very ways of thinking as those that arranged the take-over requested request… a superior life, or a re-visitation of their previous life, as Seattle's zone of affection called CHOP or CHAZ, didn't work very well.

because of seeing this endeavor at rebel self standard, and what the Seattle

Mayor portrayed as "maybe it very well may be a mid year of adoration" many presently see that the pathway to Nirvana or Utopia is a troublesome one.

his has been attempted previously, as in the Haight-Ashbury space of San Francisco in the 1960's, and the Soviet Union through the greater part of the twentieth century.

People that have seen this previously and know history and prefer the best qualities and parts of customary America know as of now, they are on the right half of history and freedom, and that America is extremely broken and useless and frantically needs assistance to stand up against new age extreme left liberal powers that try to subjugate and obliterate it.

True American loyalists know the conventional American thought of opportunity and freedom created over hundreds of years merits shielding, worth battling for, and worth securing… even from itself now and then, and the crazy desolates of extreme left oppression communist belief systems and the ruining oppression of social sensitivity, and a consistently nosy extreme left thoughts and their toadies in government that annihilate families and family esteems, yet additionally reason and long haul social practicality, if not survival.

AMERICA THE LAND OF INVENTION AND OF "THE AMERICAN DREAM"

After the Civil War, the Industrial Revolution and development blast proceeded, and America kept on developing. Straightforward things like spiked metal restrained the west, and an entire host of new innovations occurred.

merican business from these and numerous different developments blast. America came to be viewed as the place where there is fresh new chances and advancement, ultimately creating a larger number of extremely rich people than any remaining countries, totally disavowing the possibility of socialism, as socialism appallingly continues to instruct, however few appear to learn, uniformity can't be ordered by government command or control, significance must be accomplished by opportunity. So fruitful was this equation, the world paid heed. Today, the Chinese are duplicating large numbers of these perspectives at the present time, in certain cases showing improvement over were, as America fostered the blueprint.

Aside from innovation, America turned into a sanctuary for worldwide social developments of opportunity and freedom to create. The most outstanding in the nineteenth century

was the Women's development. Ladies and their difficulty everywhere, since forever ago, were looked as "the more fragile" sex, however in America, it was to be remembered they were a solitary individual, with freedoms and advantages some other resident would have. Those that battled for equity had the option to give American ladies things that ladies in different nations of the world have never had. Ladies would now have a peculiarity in that they were not property, they would have a voice and a vote, and uncommon freedom, and occupations never before accessible to ladies, and would have securities from viciousness and enslavement. The ladies' balance development took off in America like no other place.

n the late 1800 through the turn of the century, moderate developments to work on the state of all Americans additionally took off. Causes like tidying up urban communities sewer frameworks (where none had recently existed) were and seen as positive developments. Besides, moderate causes like laborers freedoms and the separation of huge incredible business restraining infrastructures that attempted to utilize their influence to control individuals and lawmakers were assaulted and separated by Trust-busting government officials like Teddy Roosevelt and the Republicans.

In this time, America and its kin were filling in abundance, information, opportunity, and way of life, and it appeared to be the remainder of the world could utilize a portion of their standards to work on their own situation... A predicament that didn't change a lot north of hundreds or now and again, a large number of years.

AMERICA SAVES THE WORLD IN THE 20TH

CENTURY

Aside from some great in some ever-evolving causes and some dynamic developments, the twentieth century saw the ascent of more dangerous and oppressive belief systems that sprang out of "moderate" thoughts. Philosophies that appeared to be great at that point... similar as our overt sensitivity of today... acquired some degree of acknowledgment, yet as these belief systems advanced, we observed these good natured philosophies at times made oppression, hopelessness, and lead to no end and destruction.

here appeared to be a connection, the more modest the reason, the better the result. The bigger the reason and the more "complete" the philosophy, the results were much of the time disastrous.

isguided "ivory tower" musings thus called "moderate" thoughts like Communism and fascism, cleared up and overwhelmed Europe. Besides, assailant types of patriotism and racial prevalence burned-through different countries, advocating their nationalistic objectives of success and control, prompting Nazism, and Japanese Imperialism.

In the mid twentieth century, Europe appeared to be bound for an incredible conflict. This conflict was stirred up by over the top

This conflict began in 1914, and America at first attempted to avoid it. It did until its boats were assaulted, and individuals killed, and organizations compromised. Besides, the Germans attempted to align themselves with Mexico and possibly use Mexico as an attack course into America.

This occasion combined with another enormous scope transport sinking causing the extraordinary loss of American life, pushed America to join the conflict in 1917.

In a straightforward expression, President Woodrow Wilson set American international strategy for over 100 years to come when he said we will battle this conflict to "Make the world safe for Democracy."

Making the world safe for popular government has been the core value from that point onward, and it has carried soundness and edification to the world, and it also

somewhat has been the core value that made America a world chief (However, this was a twofold edge sword as this approach has additionally maneuvered us into wars going from Vietnam to Middle East conflicts soon after Wilson's statement.)

With American power, entering the conflict in 1917, the Germans and their partners didn't have a potential for success, and they gave up barely a year after American soldiers began to arrive.

Despite winning World War I, "the Great War" and "The War to put to shame all other Wars" America was hesitant to partake in the harmony a short time later, and it cost us dearly.

orld War I, a conflict that was thought to end all conflicts, rather made a cruel harmony as different powers drew up the particulars of the Armistice. In the "harmony" arrangements that were marked completion the conflict, a monetary irregularity was made by pounding sanctions dropped on Germany, that they eventually couldn't pay, that aided lead by and large to a devastating worldwide Great Depression. This Depression helped fuel extremist patriot developments around the world... This may sound recognizable to individuals today.

Then as in now when industry is annihilated or on the other hand assuming positions are delivered abroad enmasse without proportional exchange or similar advantage to the country, huge joblessness results. Besides, as in this day and age, agents got inventive with monetary devices and instruments that broke the framework. This likewise occurred in 2008 with "inventive monetary instruments" that annihilated numerous property holders and families.

The over the top money of the 1920's ended up being a ticking delayed bomb very much like we see today. As the ticking delayed bomb transformed into Depression of the 1930's, these powers brought into the world of despondency and financial mayhem, made the flash for cultural change for the more terrible, and drove a few countries to revolutionary legislatures set upon development and triumph and drove these countries down a way towards war.

To help escape their monetary conditions, a few countries like Japan and Germany attacked different nations, to loot assets, open new business sectors, and develop their economies and public desires. Germany attacked places like Czechoslovakia and Poland. Meanwhile, Japan was rampaging

through China.

s occasions like the Rape of Nanking happened in China, where Japanese fighters assaulted, took, and executed thousands, America would defend China (as America consistently had supported China).

because of Japan's rough activities, America restricted oil to Japan (as America was a main provider to Japan of oil), as most economies don't work without oil Japan needed to one or the other back down or needed to challenge and stand up to America.

Japan settled on some unacceptable decision.

On December 7, 1941… A date that lives in shame… The United States was unexpectedly and intentionally assaulted, by the maritime and flying corps of Japan.

America would be doing battle, a conflict America would need to sort the world out and make alright for majority rule government, and America would come charging to the rescue.

Of the Pearl Harbor assault FDR would happen to say"

No matter what amount of time it might require for us to conquer this planned attack, the American individuals in their equitable may will win through to outright victory.

... .With trust in our military, with the unbounding assurance of our kin, we will acquire the unavoidable victory — so help us God.

On the opposite side of the Atlantic, the incomparable British Prime Minister Winston Churchill had effectively gone through his snapshot of the guard of his nation and of Western Civilization months sooner, and his enunciation of the significant of its safeguard from the powers of oppression where he announced

We will happen as far as possible. We will battle in France, we will battle on the oceans and seas, we will battle with becoming stronger noticeable all around, we will protect our island, whatever the expense might be. We will battle on the sea shores, we will battle on the arrival grounds, we will battle in the fields and in the roads, we will battle in the slopes; we will never give up, and if, which I do

not briefly accept, this island or a huge piece of it were oppressed and starving, then, at that point, our Empire past the oceans, outfitted and protected by the British Fleet, would carry on the battle, until, in God's fun time, the New World, with all its power and may, steps forward to the salvage and the freedom of the old.

This battle was hard for the British, their partner France had been crushed and taken out of the conflict, and the United Kingdom were the last country in Europe at all prepared to confront Hitler. The early pieces of the conflict went poorly for the UK, as they required American arms, American supplies, and somewhat the American Navy just to hold tight. As they battled for their endurance and the endurance of Western Civilization itself, their conflict was crushing on with no unmistakable end in sight.

With the assault of the Japanese on America, Churchill knew the New World, with all its power and may, would step forward to the salvage and the freedom of the old. Churchill's response to America entering the conflict was one of both rapture and of salvation.

Presently right now, I realized that the United States was in the

Churchill realized that America was a key country. One the world required and depended upon, none more so than Britain.

With this approaching conflict, America would be changed everlastingly and would assist with reshaping the world. America would free voices and people groups subjugated by goading belief systems of the extreme left and the extreme right that had assumed control over the world and obliterated those individuals' opportunities and lives.

People like Chinese residents hoping to be liberated from dread of the Japanese trespassers, or besieged out Londoners assaulted by the Nazi Luftwaffe, and individuals like Anne Frank a little Dutch young lady expecting her salvation from the

Nazis.

n our retaliate on Hitler and the freedom of the European mainland, it required quite a long while to collect the powers and benefits important to try and endeavor a reclaim of that European landmass. During that time, we retaliated in different areas of the planet, or sent our Air Forces to bomb Nazi industry to slow their fight.

Today, in case you go to the eighth Air Force exhibition hall in Savannah, Georgia, you can see with outright clearness the measure of penance Americans made as there are THOUSANDS of dedication plaques signifying and celebrating the huge number of Americans that passed on or were harmed or lost without a trace battling above Nazi Germany.

By the time we were prepared to mount that test, it was as yet muddled assuming we were truly prepared, and could reclaim Europe from a capably settled in Germany. The day we went, D-Day on June sixth ,1944 the climate was dreadful, air dropped troops were dissipated, a significant number of the changed tanks basic to crushing the Nazi forefront sank on the way, there were not many hole foxholes for troops to stow away in (jeez, can the Americans get a break, for what reason does the battle consistently should be so damn hard?) Nonetheless, press on they did.

Because of all the vulnerability, President Roosevelt would look for each benefit, each device, and look for each weapon, and would try to bring together and rally a country in petition for their children, their dads, and their kinsmen partaking in the Great Crusade and the attack of Europe. On a broadly communicated radio message on June 6 for the Normandy Invasion FDR would say-

"My kindred Americans:

Last evening, when I talked with you about the fall of Rome, I knew at that point that soldiers of the United States and our partners were crossing the Channel in another and more noteworthy activity. It has happened with progress accordingly far.

And thus, in this powerful hour, I request that you get together with me in prayer:

lmighty God: Our children, pride of our Nation, this day have set upon a strong undertaking, a battle to protect our Republic, our religion,

and our development, and to set free an enduring mankind. Lead them straight and valid; invigorate their arms, strength to their souls, endurance in their faith.

They will require Thy gifts. Their street will be long and hard. For the foe is solid. He might fling back our powers. Achievement may not accompany hurrying pace, however we will return over and over; and we realize that by Thy elegance, and by the nobility of our motivation, our children will win. They will be sore attempted, around evening time and by day, without rest until the triumph is won. The murkiness will be lease by commotion and fire. Men's spirits will be shaken with the savagery's of war.

For these men are recently drawn from the methods of harmony. They battle not for the desire of success. They battle to end success. They battle to free. They battle to allow equity to emerge, and resistance and kindness among all Thy individuals. They long however for the finish of fight, for their re-visitation of the shelter of home.

Some won't ever return. Embrace these, Father, and get them, Thy chivalrous workers, into Thy realm. What's more for us at home - - fathers, moms, youngsters, spouses, sisters, and siblings of valiant men overseas
- whose considerations and supplications are ever with them- - help us, Almighty God, to rededicate ourselves in restored confidence in Thee, in this hour of extraordinary sacrifice.

Many individuals have asked that I call the Nation into a solitary day of uncommon petition. But since the street is long and the craving is extraordinary, I request that our kin dedicate themselves in a duration from supplication. As we ascend to each new day, and again when every day is spent, left expressions of supplication alone all the rage, conjuring Thy help to our efforts.

Give us strength, as well - - strength in our day by day undertakings, to increase the commitments we make in the physical and the material help of our military. Furthermore let our hearts be strong, to stand by out the long struggle, to bear distresses that might come, to confer our fortitude unto our children wheresoever they may be.

And, O Lord, give us Faith. Give us Faith in Thee; Faith in our sons;

Faith in one another; Faith in our assembled campaign. Let not the insight of our soul at any point be dulled. Let not the effects of impermanent occasions, of worldly matters of however short lived second let not these hinder us in our unconquerable purpose.

With Thy favoring, we will beat the unholy powers of our adversary. Assist us with overcoming the missionaries of ravenousness and racial arrogancies. Lead us to the saving of our nation, and with our sister Nations into a world solidarity that will spell a definite harmony a harmony resistant to the schemings of dishonorable men. Also a harmony that will let all of men live in opportunity, receiving the simply benefits of their legitimate toil.

By the time America had the option to battle through to free Europe, the battle would cost countless American lives, and those troopers would happen upon wretchedness and inhumane imprisonments and utter annihilation. In this grotesqueness of war, and in their battle, it was trusted that another post-war agreement and authority would occur.

Today, we actually see that large numbers of those fallen American warriors, were not sent home, yet let go in the nations they were killed battling in, as their expensive a penance upon the special raised area of opportunity would revere them there where they died.

n a considerable lot of these European nations, each trooper's grave has a residing European support or family liable for its upkeep, and in numerous graveyards, there is as yet a holding up rundown to turn into an American grave sponsor.

After the arrivals at Normandy, America was on a pathway to triumph in World War II, as wherever American fighters went in involved Europe, mayhem would eject upon their appearance. Freedom, opportunity, and salvation was delivered.

The American military and their partners would work

everything out. In the Pacific theater, the conflict was

similarly as intense.

Americans from the get-go in the conflict needed to suffer rout in places like the Philippines, where a huge number of Americans were kidnapped and became detainees of war. In their catch, these Americans needed to persevere through the Bataan Death walk a more than 60-mile constrained walk, where they were beaten and tormented, just to be set in their imprisonment. Huge number of Americans and their Filipino partners were killed on the walk and in the subsequent jail camp and was to be one of many atrocities submitted by the Japanese during the war.

he American armed force wasn't the main gathering to endure rout right off the bat in the conflict, as the Navy had many boats sunk and taskforces obliterated from places like the Wake Island, and the Makassar Straights off Indonesia, to the Savo Islands in the Solomon Islands. The early months of the conflict were difficult for America.

After the Battle of Midway that would all change. America took on back!

At the Conflicts of the Coral Sea and Midway, the American Navy and American industry hustled to get Naval Fleets situated in the middle of the Japanese and their targets for takeover. This work again came at incredible expense for the Americans, as large number of mariners and many pilots were killed or adrift out in the ocean attempting to ward off the Japanese invasions.

With the Battle of Midway, the Americans successfully retaliated the Japanese and annihilated 4 Aircraft Carriers to the deficiency of just 1 American transporter. Without airplane and Aircraft Carriers to secure their armada, the Japanese had to withdraw and were put on edge…. . this would switch things around of the war.

and the Pacific War would turn bloodier.

Americans would need to reclaim islands to crawl nearer to Japan so they could remove their naval force and encompass their island for intrusion. In the reclaim of these islands an incredible bloodbath followed. Fights on islands like Guadalcanal, Saipan, Iwo Jima, the Philippines, Okinawa, were as hard battled and ridiculous and brutal as any fights at any point found in human history.

n the maritime skirmish of Samar in the Philippines there was the brave battle of the Naval taskforce bunch Taffy III. This fight, was the place where a couple of little and all the way out gunned American Destroyers, combat courageously until the very end and had the option to ward off immensely gigantic gunned Japanese war vessels and

weighty cruisers.

The team gathering of Taffy III was a unit of little destroyers at first dispatched to shield the arrivals in the Philippines from a submarine assault. These destroyers with their little weapons were truly not appropriate for goliath armada power commitment, as those assignments were passed on to units of airplane or ships or bigger cruisers. Destroyers with their 5-inch weapons with shells that weighed around 50 or 60 pounds were no counterpart for ships like ships whose protective layer was inches thick and whose own huge type firearms discharged shells weighing just about 2,000 pounds or more, each.

As the troop arrivals were occurring in the Philippines, to everybody's shock a tremendous Japanese naval force team shockingly showed up practically all of a sudden with their goliath warships and substantial cruisers. In any case, the destroyers of Taffy III all charged sacrificially and bravely, with uninhibited assurance, towards the gigantic Japanese Naval power and assaulted a predominantly unrivaled armada. They flooded forward to their specific obliteration and likely passing, all in their work, to save the leftover unarmed armada, and maybe great many other Americans.

Through sheer assurance and the will to battle and oppose, the gathering marvelously held off the assailants as the Japanese took unbalanced discipline from that little gallant gathering. The Japanese in their shock about the savagery of the counter-assault expected a significantly bigger gathering of Americans was coming to battle them. Subsequently, the Japanese armada turned around and withdrew regardless of overpowering prevalence and odds.

This staggering zeroed in counter-assault system was additionally executed in Europe by the Germans the clash of the Bulge, where again Americans were significantly dwarfed and would have been overpowered if not standing up and battling and flinging back the Germans that attempted to pulverize and overpower the Americans.

Neither worked.

America would ultimately win these fights and a couple of months after the fact win the war.

America in hoping to counter Adolph Hitler and Nazi endeavors to foster a nuclear weapon, beat Hitler and the Nazis in that work. America got the

bomb before Hitler or the Japanese could. With some degree of thought and debate America would utilize that bomb on Japan to assist with constraining their acquiescence. Notwithstanding killing around 200,000 individuals in these assaults, it is assessed that in utilizing the bomb, a large number of lives were saved, as America could deflect an intrusion of Japan that would have unavoidably prompted the passings of countless Americans, maybe millions, just as millions more Japanese.

How would we realize that this will generally be true?

The Department of Defense today parts with purple hearts to every one of those injured in battle. These awards were initially printed in 1945 in anticipation of the attack of Japan yet were never utilized in light of the fact that the nuclear bomb finished the conflict. Despite the fact that we have battled many conflicts since the acquiescence of Japan, (similar to Korea, Vietnam, Middle East contentions) we actually have not utilized ½ of our stockpile of Purple Hearts.

With the acquiescence of Japan, a rough and monstrous conflict was brought to an end.

THE AMERICAN STRUGGLE

These occasions recorded in World War II just start to expose the life and passing battle Americans have looked on the world's front lines to advance the reason for opportunity, freedom, and vote based system, and for the best ascribes of America that will keep going for many years and throughout the process of everything working out and of numerous generations.

Sometimes however in the American battle, America's backbone is tried, as Americans were forced to bear misfortune like 9/11. America when assaulted puts forth a valiant effort to pull together, shield, get by, hold tight, and to battle on.

U.S. Military History is packed with these models from World War II on. In the conflict we saw from the assault on Pearl Harbor, the Japanese catch of the Philippines and the subsequent Baatan demise March, the maritime Battle of Makassar Strait, American's fought gigantic chances just to lose... temporarily.

Once the pulled together, and got coordinated the result was unavoidable, however there still was a lot of penance to come.

As for that penance Americans have needed to suffer, simply check out any of our present day veteran saints who have given arms and legs, and broken bodies, and on occasion broken and broke spirits for America, as they address the penance for the best of the American thought. These American's, these saints all, with the serious pride that should be theirs to have laid so expensive a penance upon the special raised area of Freedom. A basic "Thank you for your administration" doesn't satisfactorily start to address the significance of their courageous efforts.

In battles with misfortune, and battle, America in its exemplary may hardened and retaliated against mind boggling chances and on occasion fended off overpowering assault to win, and to declare the possibility of America, a City on a Hill, a land that will make the world safe for Democracy that will acquire that inescapable triumph.

… so help us god.

THE COLD WAR STRUGGLE
AGAINST COMMUNISIM

In winning World War II, huge pieces of Europe and Asia we liberated because of America, yet some dangerous philosophies remained. In the Soviet Union, socialism was as yet flawless and presently expansionist, as it looked to rule the world. In saving the world, America understood its occupation was not finished; it would need to proceed to fight.

In the repercussions of World War II, partners became philosophical opponents, as the Soviet Union saw its pathway to accomplishing genuine Communism was through the control and oppression of the whole total populace under the framework of their own philosophical, political, and financial conviction system.

This ran totally incongruent to American thoughts of opportunity and freedom and autonomy of thought. In this philosophical conflict, a Cold War created, where there was minimal comparing shooting, however an extraordinary strained quality and deadlock as each side attempted to bring each other down in a passing battle any semblance of which the world had never known, as each side would ultimately foster an adequate number of atomic weapons to annihilate the whole planet.

Because of the dangerous force of atomic weapons, an impasse or stalemate created... a Cold War. A conflict of thoughts and of belief systems. A conflict to catch the hearts and brains of those that could be influenced.

AMERICA AFFIRMS THE RIGHT TO SELF DETERMINATION

arly in the contention, President Harry Truman would summarize America's common situation in this contention and deadlock

> *"I accept that it should be the strategy of the United States to help free people groups who are opposing endeavored enslavement by furnished minorities or by outside pressures. I accept that we should help free people groups to work out their own fates in their own way.*

his Truman principle turned into the post conflict American approach, as Europe after the conflict was attempting to recover.

THE MARSHALL PLAN

To make a post-war harmony, a harmony that was tricky after World War I, America's significance would require the reconstructing of Europe. Europe was again financially crushed by a World War, and in the repercussions of war, the survivors actually expected to eat. As there began to be dissention, and in certain spots, food revolts, the socialists increased their enlistment of followers in nations like Germany, Italy and France. As fundamental necessities like food and safe house were scant for some, individuals began searching for any political gathering that could simply convey food.

This monetary turmoil was fruitful ground for Communists and Communism, and it was clear America needed to act so their endeavors to free Europe would not all go to no end. To assist with supporting the revamping of an annihilated Europe, the USA created monetary help and backing approaches that would remake Europe as well as reshape Europe, as its high ranking representative secretary of State George C. Marshall for whom the arrangement was named for would say-

> *"The United States should do whatever it is able to do to assist in the return of normal economic health in the world, without which there can be no political stability and no assured peace."*

We now knew, especially after our post World War I experience, that when economic forces deteriorated, and caused widespread financial ruin and economic depression, it unleashed destructive political forces like Communism, Nazism, and allowed a creeping totalitarianism to develop in those nations destroyed economically.

Despite this, some nations clung to broken or defective ideologies in the post war era. Some even sought to expand their influence.

The Soviets seeking to expand their ideology took up this challenge of America. In the Soviet version of their Marshall Plan, the Soviets just kept troops and tanks, and secret police in the nations it took back from the Nazis and were in many ways worse for those countries than the Nazis were. Today, countries like the Czech Republic, have museums that chronicle both the Soviet occupation and the Nazi occupation, and draws a totalitarian equivalency between the two. Today, if you ask most Czechs, they will shockingly tell you that the communist overlord occupiers were WORSE than the Nazis!

Even though World War II had ended in an allied victory, and all other nations had de-mobilized and sent most of their armies back home to their families, the Soviets did not. The Soviets kept the nations they invaded during World War II and kept its World War II army largely intact and added nuclear weapons, weapons that liberals and communist sympathizers would steal from America and send to the Soviet Union.

The Soviet leader during the height of the Cold War was Nikita Khrushchev, and in 1956 would famously say of this competition between the Soviets and American conflicting ideologies-

Whether you like it or not, history is on our side. We will bury you.
Despite Khrushchev's assertions, America stood firm and resolute against Communism and absurdities of rampant government socialism and tyranny. America was armed and ready, like the Revolutionary War Minutemen. We challenged, confronted and in John Kennedy's words beared any burden, met any hardship, supported any friend, opposed all foes that assure the survival and the success of liberty.

This sprit was put to the test over the occupied city of Berlin.

THE BERLIN AIRLIFT

Before the end of World War II, the allied powers agreed to split up Germany into zones of occupation after the war. Berlin, as agreed to by the allied powers before World War 2 ended, was to be an occupied city by the US, UK, France, and the USSR. Berlin itself was well inside the Soviet Zone of occupation.

In 1947, the forever cheating, lying, duplicitous Soviets, like all amoral godless liberals, decided to make up their own rules and not abide by the agreements they signed up to. They informed the allied powers they were closing off road and rail access to Berlin. This included all shipments of food and medicine.

This was to put the Americans in a tough position; they could try to fight their way through to Berlin to keep the city open and supplied or surrender it altogether.

he Americans after the pleas of millions of Berliners to not to abandon them to the Soviets and communism, decided they would not abandon them in their dire hour of need. America would keep troops in Berlin, and they would also re-supply the city.......by air.

As the American Air Force reigned supreme in the post war and had many more and better planes than the Soviets, the route of access the Soviets could not cut off to Berlin was through the air.

ercedes Wild, a 7-year-old child in post-war Berlin during the Soviet blockade from June 1948 to May 1949, would tell her story about the airlift many years later, and she would say in an interview with Karl Weisel in 2008-

> *"We had little to eat," as the western section of Berlin had very little farmland. And though the Soviets tried to entice Berliners over to the eastern side with promises of food, those in the west knew better than to sacrifice their freedom.*

> *When Allied airplanes began delivering coal, food and other supplies, Wild said she was terrified bombs would once again fall on her city. "I asked my grandmother if we should go downstairs in the cellar once more, but she told me this time the planes were bringing food and coal."*

Wild described the brutal winter of 1948/49.

> *"We had no good clothes, no shoes," she remembers. "But we didn't fear the cold; we feared the Russians."*

espite the simplistic description, this effort was actually very dangerous as when an American plane crashed about 200 meters from Wild's home, killing the two pilots.

Wild knew that the flights between Berlin and other cities in Germany were only the tip of the iceberg. This was an American style logistical effort of transport and enormous planning, and execution, as "The real airlift" stretched all across the United States and the Atlantic Ocean, using airplanes, trains, trucks and ships.

Despite the dangers many pilots embraced their mission. One pilot, Lt. Gail Halvorsen, took it a step further. One day in July, he was filming plane takeoffs and landings at Tempelhof, the main landing site for the airlift. While there, he saw a group of children lined up behind one of the barbed-wire fences. He went to meet them and noticed that the children had nothing. Halvorsen remembers: "I met about thirty children at the barbed wire fence that protected Tempelhof's huge area. Many of these kids had nothing to do as many had destroyed schools and destroyed families.

Halvorson gave these kids some gum which the hungry kids LOVED and quickly demolished. The kids loved it so much some of the kids just licked the wrappers. Halvorson would recount he wanted to do more for the kids so he told them that the following day he would have enough gum for all of them, and he would drop it out of his plane on final approach.

One child asked, "How will we know it is your plane?"

Halvorsen told the kids that he would wiggle his wings on approach.

Later that night back in the west, Halversen his co-pilot, and his flight engineer pooled their candy rations for the next day's drop. Since the candy was heavy, to ensure the children were not hurt by the falling candy, Halvorsen made small parachutes out of handkerchiefs and tied them to the candy.

The next day, on final approach to landing into Templehof airfield, Halvorson saw the kids. As promised, he wiggled his wings on approach as he readied the candy for the air drop.

The kids on the ground saw the plane with the wiggling wings and pointed skyward and looked to the sky with great expectation. As he flew over the kids, out went the candy.

n the ground below, Pandemonium erupted.

Halvorson made these drops once a week for three weeks. Each week, the group of children waiting at the Tempelhof airport fence for some inexplicable reason grew larger and larger.

When word of this effort reached the airlift commander, Lieutenant General William H. Tunner, he ordered it expanded into Operation "Little Vittles." Operation Little Vittles began on September 22, 1948, and support for this effort to provide the children of Berlin with chocolate, gum, and candy grew quickly, first among Halvorsen's pilot friends, and then to the entire squadron.

As news of Operation Little Vittles reached the United States, children and candy makers from all over the US began contributing candy to the effort. By November 1948, Halvorsen could no longer keep up with the amount of candy and handkerchiefs being sent from across America.

In total, it is estimated that Operation "Little Vittles" was responsible for dropping over 23 tons of candy from over 250,000 parachutes.

Halvorsen himself became known by many nicknames to the children of Berlin as "Uncle Wiggly Wings", or the "Chocolate Uncle", and also the "Chocolate Flier".

One of those children on the receiving end of those candy drops was that 7-

year-old already mentioned, Mercedes Wild. Mercedes, having lost her father during World War II, was at those candy drops. She would say she looked to Halvorsen as a surrogate dad.

> *"My father was also a pilot in World War II and he (went missing) early in the war. My mother and I didn't know what happened to him. ... The chocolate uncle became a symbol of my father."*

In 1997, during the 50th anniversary of the airlift at Temploehof Airport in Berlin, Wild was invited on stage alongside Gail Halvorsen and American President Bill Clinton, where she had the honor to say-

> *hank you on behalf of the people of Berlin. "Without the help of the Americans (and the Allies), I wouldn't be here,..... I wouldn't be alive to enjoy the freedom you brought to us Germans."*

With Great American efforts like the Marshal Plan and the Berlin Airlift, America has always been recognized as the greatest humanitarian nation on earth, but as America was to find out, they could not win the Cold War on airlifting food alone.

This Cold War confrontation also spread to Asia as in Korea when in 1950 communist armies from North Korea invaded South Korea. The "incredibly terrible and racist nation" (as liberals cry about) the United States of America, went to protect Asians in South Korea that were threatened by communist invaders from the north.

As Americans fought and died in frozen places like the Chosin Reservoir where the 1st Marine Division battled perhaps more than 250,000 Chinese soldiers, American and the American military was once again put to the test.

"The incredibly racist nation" of America (as liberals assert) would also go on to defend Asians in South Vietnam…and "The incredibly racist nation" America would decades later protect Muslims being threatened with genocide
in the Balkans in the 1990's and protect middle eastern Kuwaitis and Saudi Arabia from Sadam Hussien, and protect blacks in Somalia from starvation and warlords, and many other people of different colors and faiths.

In defending so many people of color and faiths I will presume the liberals are liars or misinformed as it is clear America is NOT "The incredibly racist nation" they want to label us as, as America has stood up to evil and defended much of the world against that evil no matter the color or faith.

is-informed liberals somehow fail to understand (thanks to our broken schools and school systems and liberal academia) that America and the American military are in fact great and have saved the world…repeatedly. Saved the world of all peoples, all faiths, all ideologies, and of all ethnicities.

It was not just a white military that did this, but ALL groups in America have a legacy of contribution to America's saving the world.

hese groups contributions could not be diminished despite segregation attempts by Democratic politicians and Democratic party policies.

Groups like the legendary black Tuskegee Airmen – A Fighter squadron in World War II of black pilots that never lost a bomber being shot down while THEY were escorting them over Germany.

he American 442nd Infantry Regiment - A fighting unit composed almost entirely of second-generation American soldiers of Japanese ancestry (Nisei) who fought in Europe during World War II, and were one of the most highly decorated units in the entire war.

The Windtalkers – Native American's helped build this great nation in helping the pilgrims and early settlers. In addition, Native American troops were instrumental in the War in the Pacific, as they served on the front lines, as their communication to artillery strikes and troop movements was as indispensible as their code was unbreakable.

he WACs' – a Women's only pilot group during World War II that served moving military aircraft to the front lines and kept our troops critically supplied in the war effort.

Even back during the Revolutionary War, Crispus Attucus, a free black

man, was the first American killed fighting against the British during the American Revolution.

America's military history is beyond great in victory, in defeat, and in struggle. From Normandy to Desert Storm, to the Battle of Midway, to Afghanistan, America's battlefield history is beyond glorious, and has been a liberating force for good and for freedom.

American relief efforts like the Peace Corps (started under President John F

Kennedy), and all the American led humanitarian efforts also show Americas non-military greatness as well, as "racist and terrible" America has contributed more humanitarian aid and relief than any other nation on earth.

A WAR OF IDEOLOGIES

Aside from bloody Cold War proxy fights like the Korean or Vietnam War, some of these battles in the Cold War were fought without guns; like the race to space, or the rebuilding of Europe after the war.

In 1980 another one of these ideological Cold War struggles unexpectedly played out in small town in Lake Placid, New York in that year's Winter Olympics.

he resulting highlight of those 1980 Olympics was of all things a hockey game. This game was one where a bunch of 22-year-old American hockey amateurs, confronted the then best hockey team in the world (and maybe the most dominant hockey team of all time) from the USSR.

In an effort to promote their Communist system as a shining example of their superiority over capitalism and the west, the Soviets put tremendous effort and resource into their Olympians, especially their national hockey team; a team that represented their system, their nation, and their collective national identity. Their focused efforts at presentation and putting on a facade or false front worked very well, even if their ideological and economic system did not.

he Soviets would promote themselves on a world stage in events like the Olympics, in which they would create super athletes that were drugged on steroids, put through grueling training from the times they were identified as

athletic talents as young children, and poured enormous resources into sports programs...all so that Communism would be perceived as the best societal system.

These facades were effective, as many people believed the Soviet propaganda. The simplest and most deceiving of Soviet facades were on full display when I went to Berlin in post Cold War 1990 and 91, as I could plainly see on full display bombed out buildings from almost 45 years earlier that were STILL bombed out shells but had new fake fronts or facades that pointed west, so that West Berliners might think the Soviet sector was more prosperous than it actually was.

As for more complex facades the Soviets put on, their space program was pretty good, as it was pretty real. The Soviets had achievements greater than the Americans did early in the space race, and tried to show off to the rest of the world the greatness of their "Soviet System".….while the rest of the Soviet economy and population suffered, and was nowhere near as successful as their space program, it looked good from the outside.

Furthermore, another great Soviet facade was in their Olympic sports programs. Just like Hitler, the Soviets wanted to show the "greatness of their system" through sports. In this effort the Soviets produced some dominant teams and athletes.

So good was the 1980 Soviet hockey team that they had on occasion utterly demolished and embarrassed NHL All Star teams in exhibition games; the last NHL challenge game they played before the 1980 Olympics, being 6-0 blow out Soviet win over the NHL All Stars, an NHL All-Star team laden with future Hall of Famers!

owever, when that same Soviet came to the Olympics in 1980, they faced a different hockey team. This time without professional NHL hockey All-Stars and Hall of Famers, the Soviets would face a team of amateur volunteers merely with the words U.S.A. on their jerseys, and something else would happen. In this, the 1980 American Olympic Hockey Team revealed themselves as a group of focused, fearless, and intense warriors with ice skates.

The Americans, though not highly ranked entering the 1980   Olympic

tournament, had played tremendously in their run up to the medal round in the Olympics, crushing the second ranked Czechoslovaks, and tying the third ranked Swedes, winning the rest of their qualifying games, and drew the attention of a nation.

he stage was set.

In a game Sports Illustrated would eventually name the greatest athletic event of the 20th Century, these American amateurs would battle the Soviets for a chance to play for an Olympic Gold Medal.

Though not scheduled originally to play each other, the two teams would meet in the medal round, and in the media's explosion and highly charged 48 hours in the run up to the game, each team knew the stakes involved- a chance at Olympic Gold.

The challenge was daunting as the Americans were much younger, much less experienced, much less talented, and much less poised, as the USSR had so much big game experience against the best competition the world could assemble against the Soviets, and the Soviets crushed them.

Nonetheless, the Americans had prepared ferociously for months leading up to their showdown game, and in their chance to translate hard work and a brilliant game plan developed by their coach, Herb Brooks, into success; they showed up for themselves and for America in that game.

As the game got underway, the Soviets scored first. As the game progressed, the Americans repeatedly had to come from behind against the Soviets. The Soviets would score, then the Americans countered.

s the game progressed further, the Soviets just could not break or dispirit the Americans or put them away like a bunch of weak pampered NHL All- Stars. The Americans players themselves had to fight to rally their own home crowd, as there was a quiet nervousness and unease, but the Americans fought on. After tying the game for the 3rd time, the American crowd exploded. The fearsome, unflintinching, emotionless Soviets uncharacteristically were being shaken to their core and started looking at each other.

The Soviets had earlier been rattled when they replaced their   starting

goaltender earlier in the game when he gave up a break away goal with just :02 seconds on the clock before the end of the 1st period to the scrappy never-say-die American team. Now with more energy and crowd noise the behind the Americans, team USA surged again...The Americans were now soaring in their epic fight for the ages.

Almost as quick as the game restarted after their 3rd goal, the Americans quickly broke through the Soviet defense and scored ANOTHER goal. This goal was scored by their team captain Mike Eruzione, whose name in Italian means eruption, and he delivered just that.

andemonium...........Pandemonium............utter Pandemonium.....

The American's took the lead for the first time.

The Soviets lost their lead and were losing their composure to the never-say-die Americans. The Soviets, now behind for the first time, furiously tried to come.

They could not.

As the game clock ticked down to zero, TV game announcer Al Michaels typified the disbelief when he exclaimed "Do you believe in Miracles?....YES!!!!

The Americans at last won that heavenly day over the Soviets by a score of 4-3 and it would prompt a possible Gold Medal win for the Americans. Group USA was driven by mentor Herb Brooks, who knew something about battle, as he was the last player cut from the Gold Medal winning 1960 Olympic group, (that additionally furious the Soviets in that year as well). It was thought mentor Brooks was driven by that inability to make a solid effort to cut out his own hockey story and accomplish his own gold decoration. He and his group of American symbols did as such magnificently and forever.

Yes, Herb Brooks and that group are awesome of American exertion and assurance and cooperation... It was as extraordinary of a success as it was an approval of our aggregate American personality and character.

As for the Olympics, obviously everybody knows which country on Earth has won the most Olympic decorations ever... and that is The United States of

America, of course.

As the 1980's proceeded, Ronald Reagan was chosen President supplanting an exceptionally liberal and extremely maladroit Jimmy Carter. America was battling financially in the 1970's and under Regan's optimism, and forcefulness of character out of nowhere refound itself and its fate. Business returned, and an arms move toward challenge and face the Soviets helped Make America Great Again in the 1980's. America delivered innovative miracle weapons the Soviets couldn't copy and emptied colossal financial assets into to attempt to counter. As Reagan proceeded with his endeavors to challenge and go up against the extremist Soviets, his residency as President finished up in provoking the Soviets to coordinate with our development, and our resurgence, and our opportunity, and our lifestyle. Bravely, jokingly, and harshly Ronald Regan moved his Soviet partner to free the oppressed in Eastern Europe and at a discourse in Berlin he roared –

> *We invite change and receptiveness; for we accept that opportunity and security go together, that the development of human freedom can just fortify the reason for world peace.*

> *There is one sign the Soviets can make that would be undeniable, that would progress significantly the reason for opportunity and peace.*

> *General Secretary Gorbachev, in case you look for harmony, in case you look for thriving for the Soviet Union and Eastern Europe, in case you look for advancement, come here to this door. Mr Gorbachev, open this entryway. Mr Gorbachev...*

> *Mr. Gorbechev, TEAR DOWN THIS WALL!*

To which under a year after the fact, that divider did for sure come tumbling down. A divider, a Berlin Wall, was put up to keep individuals in, to secure degenerate philosophies, similar to a present day "place of refuge", and keep them subjugated, as the East was losing its generally skilled and fit individuals toward the west before the divider was built.

Today, there is more contention with dividers, as it is obvious to everything is that we have a country too liberal thus giving we currently need to assemble a divider to keep multitudes of individuals out, multitudes of individuals that would overpower us and our

capacity to help existing Americans. Wherein the Soviets constructed dividers to keep individuals in, we need to fabricate dividers to keep individuals out... .the irony.

merica's triumph in its Cold War battle is additionally to a great extent owing to its will to persevere through and experience those difficulties John Kennedy traces. In those difficulties, however, America accomplished significance and greatness. Now and again, this seriousness gushed out over on the combat zone, yet through occasions like the rush to the moon, or even in minuscule spots like Lake Placid, New York.

American purpose, fortitude, and lifestyle eventually pushed the Soviet Union to the brink of collapse, and the Soviet Empire fell. Europe was liberated, and the Second World War at long last reached a conclusion. A piece of the incongruity is that the Soviet Unions breakdown likewise freed Russia from its own detaining belief system, and a large number of Russians and Eastern Europeans were liberated there too… .all without open fighting and the demise and obliteration that a conflict would have brought.

America assisted with liberating the Russian individuals without a shot being fired.

AMERICA AND ITS CHANGING CULTURE

America is a social power, as America is productive in motion pictures, music, and literature.

America has created some incredible and rousing music, and craftsmanship, and films like Star Wars or Forrest Gump or Hoosiers. These mix the spirit and inspire.

However, it likewise ought to be noticed that Hollywood since the 1960's had additionally become hazier, and a large part of the world had impeded or restricted an amazing measure of the substance they have marked social pollution.

As numerous dissidents like to call attention to (and in light of current circumstances) natural contamination that "Huge Business" dumps into the climate as things like poisonous slop, is destructive to people. In any case, Liberals appear to ignore the CULTURAL POLLUTION "Huge Hollywood" siphons out that obliterates the spirit and toxins the brain and is just about as destructive as ecological pollution.

Hollywood would counter that large numbers of its creations extended people groups psyches and thinking, this is valid, however it likewise changed socially during the violent 60's; a period that delivered and celebrated disastrous screw-ups… .and misfortune. A portion of the motion pictures however conveyed this somewhat further by enjoying that antagonism, and childishness, and haziness, and now and again a glorification of savagery, drug use, hyper-sexualized and misanthropic guilty pleasure to the detriment of others, and a hug of the new skeptical culture creating since the 1960's.

urthermore, Liberals that rule Hollywood today will quite often twist history, such as assuming praise for things like the Civil Rights Movement. This is silly. The battle for Civil Rights is a piece of the American battle, yet the human battle since man imagined fire, and Republicans were in reality in front of gatherings like Hollywood, and the scholarly world, and surprisingly the Democrats in this.

Liberals in their dream of Hollywood creation, and fake grant coming from the scholarly community, accept that main ethnic minorities needed to "battle in America" or "battle for their social equality." Well, the pioneers needed to battle for their social liberties. Ladies needed to battle for their social equality. Irish

and Italians needed to battle for their social equality. The Chinese chipping away at the rail lines in America needed to battle for their social liberties. This is a human struggle.

In this human battle, Republicans and Democrats differ on who is more instrumental in the Civil Rights endeavors. Oftentimes this Civil privileges battle is placed into a class fighting setting by Democrats, as regularly the core of the matter concerning what Republicans and Democrats can't help contradicting is the manner by which to accommodate poor people. Conservatives, who trust in opportunity and autonomy and restricted government dread that out and out government giveaways will make reliance, as individuals will not work.

Democrats like it when individuals don't work... it makes individuals subordinate ... . subject to Democrats.

Not to say Democrats have done nothing right, this would not be valid, in light of the fact that America has a totally bigoted history... . that is additionally false. Leftists, Hollywood, and indeed, even nonconformists, have benefited a few things, some GREAT things, yet never appear to give moderates or Republicans a similar credit.   In this book I give numerous instances of Democrats and Democratic Presidents that have said or done extraordinary things, as I likewise give numerous instances of Republican Presidents that have said or done incredible things. Notwithstanding, the scholarly community today, contaminated by a Marxist build, will in general excuse or disregard the commitments of Conservatives or Republicans.

Republicans in the account of who is great and awful are not perceived for their commitments to Civil Rights. This is seen on the least difficult premise, in that during the Civil War the Union Army was coordinated by the Republican President, Abraham Lincoln, who likewise looked to utilize that de-isolated armed force to free the slaves.

Moving forward on schedule, it was President Woodrow Wilson, a Democrat, 50 years after Lincoln, that re-isolated the Federal government and armed force. As America had an isolated Army in World War I and World War II. It was likewise a Democrat, Franklin D Roosevelt, that didn't coordinate the military during World War II whenever he had the chance to do so.

If discussing the Black social equality battle in America, the main motivation blacks are held during these time in their battle for social equality is they are the

nonconformists greatest and most solid democratic square, and liberal Democrats need to keep blacks on their liberal manor as far as might be feasible. Paying off them with cash, government giveaways, and making an "us versus them" account assists nonconformists with keeping control... .and blacks deciding in favor of Democrats, as downtown areas have been constrained by Democrats for generations!

It is crystal clear dissidents and Democrats use blacks to acquire power... .to keep power they would need to keep downtown in confusion and neediness. Drugs, broken families, helpless tutoring, and absence of discipline are the Democrats alarming heritage in the internal city.

As Democrats have held blacks down for ages from servitude (as the Democrats opposed Republican endeavors to free the slaves), to Jim Crow (Democrat arrangements), to the KKK (Largely Democrats), to Segregation (Democrats), to Liberal Democrat "gifts" that annihilated dark families and kept blacks dependant, blacks would have needed to battle to defeat for decades.

In their battle, at times blacks would require a legend to help them.

MARTIN LUTHER KING AND THE MEMPHIS SANITATION WORKER STRIKE

1968 got going like each and every year during the 1960's, yet the tone of the public discussion and discourse was beginning to increase as there were a few combining powers. An undeniably disliked conflict in Vietnam that were sending more American children home in banner hung coffins every week, and 1968 was additionally a political decision year. Set against this scenery of disturbance, there was an always expanding Civil Rights development in which was stirring things up as well.

In February 1968, the Civil Rights center moved to Memphis and occasion that was starting to get steam there, in an approaching sterilization laborer strike. Memphis, as a large part of the American South, had a past filled with isolation and unreasonable treatment for blacks. In the times of Jim Crow Laws, Blacks had their battle, and started to push for equivalent treatment. Back then, Blacks were prohibited from associations and paid considerably less than whites were. These disinfection laborers, junk men, individuals that took what was undesirable and disposed of, and to those individuals was garbage.

The specialists that gathered and unloaded this decline were not trash. They were men, and the sparkle that lighted the strike was incited by the killing of two specialists in a garbage compactor.

Martin Luther King saw what was happening in Memphis and concluded he would go there to help these men in their endeavors to work on their lives and stand up against a wrecked framework. Nonetheless, before Martin Luther King even withdrew to Memphis, his plane had a bomb danger brought in, and that made an agitating tone for the excursion. In this excursion, there some nearby partners that revealed that he had an incredible disquiet on that outing, one they hadn't saw previously. Some idea he may have been sick for a couple of days, others would propose he anticipated extraordinary peril.

Regardless, his life in the Civil Rights period was a demonstration of mental fortitude, and of battle, and of significance consistently, as brutality and demise dangers became ordinary for Martin and his family.

n April 3, 1968, Martin Luther King would have the chance to addresses individuals from the disinfection laborers that were striking, and Martin would deliver a discourse that would reverberate through American history right up 'til today and will long be recalled through the ages.

> *And then, at that point, I got to Memphis. Furthermore some started to say the dangers... or then again talk about the dangers that were*

out. What might befall me from a portion of our wiped out white siblings? All things considered, I don't have the foggiest idea what will happen now. We have some troublesome days ahead. Yet, it doesn't make any difference with me now. Since I've been to the mountaintop.

And I wouldn't fret. Like anyone, I might want to carry on with a long life. Life span has its place. In any case, I'm not worried about that at this point. I definitely need to do God's will. What's more He's permitted me to go up to the mountain. Furthermore I've investigated. Furthermore I've seen the Promised Land. I may not arrive with you. Yet, I need you to know this evening, that we, as a group, will get to the Promised Land! As I'm glad, tonight.

... .I'm not stressed over anything!
... .I'm not dreading any man!
... My eyes have seen the wonder of the happening to the Lord!

This intensely introduced discourse unquestionably proposed hints of Moses driving the Israelites to the incline of the guaranteed land, and like Moses, Martin Luther King would not be permitted by God to enter that guaranteed land, as the following day Martin Luther King's splendid existence of boldness was doused as he was killed while remaining on the gallery of Lorraine Motel in Memphis.

n the consequence of his shooting, there is a notable image of his consultants calling attention to police, the housetop where they accepted the shots came from, and along these lines guided the way toward their salvation, through the personalities of those that feared them, and the dread of blacks as a general rule, just due to the shade of their skin.

Today, the Lorraine Motel stays, as the now home of the National Civil Rights Museum. If at any point there had a place an American on Mount Rushmore that was not a President, it would effectively be Martin Luther King. Martin Luther King helped push a country ahead with a subject of peacefulness and set America on a course towards something better, something better without himself, then, at that point, for his kids. He also would say prior in 1963-

I have a fantasy that my four young kids will one day live in a country where they won't be decided by the shade of their skin, yet by the substance of their character.

Rest in harmony and God favor you, Martin Luther, thank you for your commitment to America and to its mankind, and to all of humankind. So amazing was Martin Luther King's voice, both President Trump and Vice President Pence would make journeys to Martin Luther King's commemoration on his birthday... regularly to little show by a philosophically and fiscally bad, exploitative, and broken American press and media that needs to pass judgment on individuals exclusively by the shade of their skin.

AMERICA; OVERCOMING

STRUGGLES AND DISSENTION, WITH HOPE
, OPTIMISM, HARD WORK, AND EFFORT

In the awfulness of Martin Luther King's demise, America detonated. 1968 was a year like no other in American history. Very little was great occurring in America, as a large number of its young were sadly maneuvered into a conflict in Vietnam; an intermediary battle for battling the horrible thought of Communism. The expense of this conflict was in some cases many youthful Americans being killed every week, uproars and flames in American urban communities were turning out to be more ordinary, grounds were beating out of resentment, dread, and dissent. America required something great to happen.

In 1968, along the bank of Florida, something great was occurring. Something that was a long time in the making.

John Kennedy, similar to Martin Luther King, was killed in an America that was turning out to be more tumultuous and more rough consistently. Prior to John Kennedy's death, he had publically set out America upon the aspiring objective of setting a man on the moon before the decade's over. This hierarchical exertion was assembled under the National Air and Space Administration or NASA and notwithstanding a few early triumphs and "small steps," the assignment of getting into space and to the moon was an undeniably challenging one, both mechanically and strategically. This, as the suggestions of the Cold War particularly became an integral factor, as we dashed the Soviets to be the primary country to achieve this feat.

In a discourse John Kennedy gave on September 12, 1962 at Rice University, a discourse that was generally credited with setting up an objective and a course of events for Americans space exertion, President Kennedy would say-

> *This nation was vanquished by the individuals who pushed ahead - thus will space.*
>
> *William Bradford, talking in 1630 of the establishing of the Plymouth Bay Colony, said that generally incredible and respectable activities are went with extraordinary troubles, and both should be enterprised*
>
> *and overwhelmed with liable courage...*
>
> *...*
>
> *e decide to go to the moon in this decade and do different things, not on the grounds that they are simple, but since they are hard, in light of the fact that that objective will serve to arrange and quantify the best of our energies and abilities, since that challenge is one that we will acknowledge, one we are reluctant to defer, and one which we expect to win... ...*
>
> *.Many years prior the incomparable British pilgrim George Mallory, who was to pass on Mount Everest, was inquired as to for what reason did he need to climb it. He said, "In light of the fact that it is there." Well, space is there, and we will climb it, and the moon and the planets are there, and new expectations for information and harmony are there. Also, consequently, as we set forth we ask God's approval on the most risky and hazardous and most noteworthy experience on what man has ever embarked.*

John Kennedy was right.

The excursion which America was leaving on was not a simple one, as from the get-go in the space program, many test rockets exploded on the platform or not long after takeoff, giving a feeling of how perilous the entire undertaking was. As the Apollo program advanced, there were a few other narrow escapes with calamity, until January 27, 1967, when three American Astronauts, Gus Grissom, Ed White, and Roger Chaffee were killed in a fire in a trial of the Apollo 1 mission. This grievous fire put the program in a difficult spot numerous months and gave both reflection and soul looking for NASA and its designers, and its providers and project workers, yet America pushed on.

As future American President Ronald Regan would propose after a future space calamity in the Space Shuttle Challenger that-

> *Sometimes, when we try the impossible, we miss the mark. Be that as it may, we should get ourselves again and go ahead notwithstanding the agony... ..We recollect the pioneers of a previous century, and the tough spirits who took their families and the possessions and set out into the boondocks of the American West. Regularly, they met with horrible difficulty. Along the Oregon Trail you can in any case see the grave markers of the people who fell coming. Yet, anguish just prepared them to the excursion ahead.*

And ahead the American space program squeezed. In the sad fire, there was a consistent soul among numerous at NASA that would do this; they would be the first, and regardless, they would do this for the space explorers that lost their lives, and for John Kennedy. These Astronauts and this space race provided America with a feeling of trust and hopefulness, which had consistently been endemic in the American soul. At the point when this was intertwined with their persistent effort and aggregate soul, the moon abruptly turned into a ton closer. Nearer to Florida, not the Soviet Union.

Though the Apollo program was slowed down after the fire to concentrate on what occurred, the Apollo program actually squeezed forward. Starting reestablished in 1968, a few Apollo missions would be dispatched that would give different demonstrating trial of the frameworks, from soaring up to earth circle to the affirmation that the lunar module worked, to a test mission to guarantee the capacity of us to really circle around the moon. Apollo 8 would be that mission to approve the capacity of a monitored module to circle the moon.

With this trying jump forward mission, NASA was presently certain they could strikingly cut time off other test and affirmation arrangements, as a lunar circle mission was climbed in this step succession. This jump ahead would interestingly, give America the lead in the space race, this as the Soviets had ALWAYS held the lead in the space race since the dispatched the initial satellite Sputnik into space in 1957, and accordingly could basically guarantee both an innovative and philosophical lead over America. The Soviets were first to send a satellite into space, the Soviets were first to send a man into space, the Soviets were first to space walk, it appeared to be the Soviets were quick to do everything in space habitually getting us off guard showing the world their mechanical predominance. After Apollo 8, they couldn't guarantee a first, as America would be quick to take space travelers around the moon. This excursion would show the world and permit America to take a goliath lead in innovation. Apollo 8 would be an approval of the direction of America and of American technology.

For this necessary jump in innovation, NASA would create the Saturn V rocket to get them there. In the American Saturn V, this fantastic piece of designing outperformed all Russians endeavors in innovation, as the Saturn V was the aftereffect of the magnificent American assembling area and the blossoming American mechanical area. The Saturn V program required, and thus

created, progressed metallurgy, high innovation F-1 motors, progressed streamlined exploration, high innovation route and direction frameworks, high innovation life emotionally supportive networks, high innovation progressed PCs, and jumps in the new study of programming improvement … inconceivable designing achievements borne of … well … rocket science.

They were dashing the Soviet Union whose Saturn V contender the N-1, was an unexpected idea in comparison to the Saturn V, and thought to be more solid, the Soviets knew this outing to the moon would, in actuality, be an extremely challenging assignment. The Soviets discovered structure rockets to circle the Earth was simple; building rockets sufficiently amazing to convey men to the moon and back was something else entirely game. The Soviets had a few test-dispatches of their N-1 rocket before the Americans were set to go to the moon. They all exploded. The blasts were so amazing they equaled the size of a little atomic blast. The Soviets realized they were in a tough situation, they realized they were being overwhelmed by a resurgent and excited America charging to the moon.

In America, the scene was starting to set up, and that energy was obvious. To battle the Soviets and their innovation, the Americans depended on designers and researchers who were predominantly younger than 40, and a decent level of them under 30. This was a young exertion contained a large number of the best and most splendid of America, of America's "most prominent age." This energetic richness would show itself at dispatches, as following quite a while of work, that energetic extravagance and energy would show itself as "Go fever" which would assume control over the now renamed Kennedy dispatch complex. Before each mission dispatch, the calls were almost indistinguishable. Latest possible moment checks were made of frameworks to the Flight Director before dispatch, and the designer or administrator liable for the different framework availability would say during the commencement cycle whether or not they were prepared for dispatch and flight. On occasion, the fervor was clear as the interjection in the agreed reactions demonstrated. In the approach dispatch, a little part of the last-minute preflight check sequencing discussion between the regulators may go as follows-

ooster – Go Retro
– Go flight!
Guidance-We are go flight!
Control – Go flight

Ecom – Go!
ap com - GO!
aunch control, this is Houston we are GO for launch!

early all regulators would uproariously, as though egotistically and gladly, articulate their availability, their fervor, their excitement at the cycle, as the monstrosity of their main goal dashing to the sky was exceptionally invigorating. It was on occasion extraordinary humankind pushing otherworldly technology.

With this air, Apollo 8 was dispatched from Cape Kennedy on December 21, 1968, and during its drawn out mission, its lunar circle would match with Christmas Eve. As 1968 was one of the absolute most savage and violent years in American history; a conflict in Vietnam, social equality dissents, various uproars, with a few urban communities altogether consumed in these mobs. Also, there were various political deaths that included Martin Luther King, and Robert Kennedy. For sure, 1968 was pretty much as terrible as any year in American history. Be that as it may, with NASA, here was a chance for them to show America and its most desirable characteristics,

characteristics how its innovation couldn't just bind together a huge number of designers, administrators, and Aerospace laborers yet additionally join a nation.

After dispatch, the goliath, extraordinarily mechanical, and massively amazing Saturn V rocket copied off and disposed of layers of the boat in stages, until what was left was the excess little Command Module. Apollo 8 was in transit off to the moon! Along these lines, similar to the Pioneers that initially got comfortable America, the Apollo 8 Astronauts played out their excursion and experience into the relative obscure in a tiny boat a long way from home and security, in a now lunar orbiter a lot more modest in size than the Mayflower.

This boat would arrive at lunar circle on Christmas Eve 1968.

pollo 8 was effectively embedded into lunar circle, and its space travelers – Frank Borman, Jim Lovell, and Bill Anders – then, at that point, turned into the primary people to circle a different universe. These three men at over a quarter million miles away were as distant and as separated as any people had at any point been from Earth, and from other human beings.

One of the allocated assignments of the space travelers on this mission was to lead a live transmission from lunar circle. This astounding transmission and

innovative accomplishment would become one of the greatest evaluated American TV occasions ever. Notwithstanding the crowd in America, it would likewise be broadcast to a huge number of individuals all over the planet who felt a comparable human association and pride, one that America more than once conveyed to the remainder of the whole world.

As their order module cruised over the lunar surface, they were passed on to their own gadgets with respect to what they needed to communicate. Prior to departure, they concurred that it would be proper to peruse from the book of Genesis, the establishment of three of the biggest religions in America-Christianity, Judaism, and Islam. This was suitable as they had traveled to the sky and had a one of a kind point of view of creation no other human had at any point had, as they had the option to glance back at the Earth and reaffirm theirs and Earth's position in the universe; thus, they would peruse from the book.

Lunar Module pilot William Anders was quick to peruse for the transmission sent from the sky, and he started –

"For every one individuals on Earth the group of Apollo 8 has a message we might want to send you".

> *"at the outset, God made the paradise and the Earth. Furthermore the Earth was without structure and void, and dimness was upon the substance of the deep.*
>
> *And the Spirit of God moved upon the essence of the*
>
> *waters. Furthermore God said, Let there be light: and*
>
> *there was light.*
>
> *And God saw the light, that it was great: and God partitioned the light from the darkness."*

nd the three daring Astronauts, similar to forlorn fighters in a foxhole hazardously gambling lives for America, taken off discreetly in circle around moon with motors off not knowing for certain if they could restart for their excursion home back to Earth.

Despite all depictions, few can sufficiently envision the work and the penance America, and the American country attempted to get these three men just to that point.

Apollo 8 Command Module Pilot (and inevitable Apollo 13 authority) Jim Lovell was the close to peruse, and he said:

> *"And God called the light Day, and the obscurity he called Night. What's more the evening and the morning were the principal day. Furthermore God said, Let there be an atmosphere amidst the waters, and let it partition the waters from the waters. Furthermore God made the atmosphere and separated the waters which were under the atmosphere from the waters which were over the atmosphere: and it was so.*
>
> *nd God called the atmosphere Heaven. Furthermore the evening and the morning were the second day."*

Mission Commander Frank Borman was straightaway, and he read:

"And God said, Let the waters under the sky be assembled unto one spot, and let the dry land show up, and it was so. Furthermore God called the dry land Earth, and the assembling of the waters called the Seas, and God saw that it was good."

"And from the group of Apollo 8, we close with great evening; best of luck, a Merry Christmas, and God favor every one of you.... All of you on the great Earth."

In this American second, our innovation and our mankind merged, there was no Tower of Babel second where human pride and over the top arrogance commended in their human accomplishment and excused God as being pointless, America was, absolutely for this second, one country under God, and indivisible.

These valiant American Astronauts, explorers and investigates into the most unfathomable piece of room man had at any point dared to date, had without a doubt as future President Ronald Reagan portrayed the future fearless NASA Astronauts of the Space Shuttle Challenger almost 20 years after the fact. "slipped the morose obligations of Earth and contacted the substance of God."

- - - - - - - - - - - - - -

pollo 8 would return effectively to Earth a couple of days after the fact, and a short

while after they arrived on Earth, they additionally arrived on the front of Time Magazine as Time "Men of the Year." NASA was bringing together a formerly broken and isolated country and aided in mending its wounds.

This recuperating would finish 7 months after the arrival of Apollo 8, and NASA would make it so.

On July 20, 1969, Apollo 11 would rehash Apollo 8's test excursion to the moon. Notwithstanding, this time it would land on the outer layer of the moon and understand the zenith of NASA and America's efforts.

Americans Neil Armstrong and Buzz Aldrin would stroll upon that moon and would establish a banner … . The American banner… .and would do as such for the sake of the multitude of countries of Earth.

They had achieved John Kennedy's goal.

America. In the midst of harmony and solace, our most exceedingly awful human characteristics will quite often come out, yet in the midst of difficulty, challenge, and emergency, our most desirable characteristics through to the surface and make themselves obvious, as it unmistakably did with our excursion into space and to the moon.

Furthermore, in this "Space Race" we would see it would produce a mechanical and logical insurgency in America the impacts of which would be felt for ages on the way. From the beginning of the space race came headways and future ventures in space investigation and satellite innovation, yet progressions in science, hardware, PC innovation, aviation innovation, metallurgy, plastics, and composite turn of events. The impacts of which are progressing right up 'til today to the advancement and added solace of our lives.

A HISTORY THAT CANNOT BE REVISED

There is no doubt that terrible things occurred in America's past as dissidents love to grumble about. In any case, when irate disdain filled and bigoted nonconformists that perpetrate wrongdoings themselves of uproars and viciousness against honest individuals' shops and stores, or appreciate killing unborn infants, or ingesting huge loads of medications (that fuel the narco-wars south of the line that eventually cause the passings of a huge number of individuals) they accept that they are independently honorable. Normal individuals (clearly not nonconformists) need to ask is it countries or individuals and human instinct that cause a significant number of the problems?

Today, negative revisionist student of history narrators that search for the awful in all things, or attempt to criticize, lessen, and excuse America and American achievements. Liberal revisionist Historians attempt to reduce Americas place in world history. In any case, they can't briefly honestly reject that America was and is, truth be told, and for sure extraordinary, and did incredible things, and that America is, indeed, the best country in mankind's set of experiences. We are largely relatives of these people who assembled this incredible country that lopsidedly formed present day mankind's set of experiences and whose endeavors and soul saved the world... .repeatedly.

s America, or would it be advisable for us to say certain individuals in America have done awful, If America itself is so terrible what might have been the world without America?

Over the process of everything working out and over numerous ages America and Americans have saved the world as only a couple of the things they have done incorporate

- Stood up for the Chinese when Japan was rampaging through the Rape of Nanking killing hundreds of thousands in the 1930's.
- Fought World War II and liberated Europe and the Pacific and freed the enslaved and imprisoned in the 1940's.
- After the war, fed and saved Europe with the Marshall Plan
- Fought to protect the Koreans, and Asian people, in the 1950's, and fought (though unsuccessfully) to protect the South Vietnamese from communist aggression in the North.
- Fed starving Somalis in the 1990's.
- Stopped a racial genocide and ethnic cleansing of Muslims in the

Balkans in the 1990's.

If America is so "bigot" for what reason did they defend, and battle for, and secure and feed these ethnic gatherings and ethnic people?

As George Bailey discovered in the film It's a Wonderful Life, what might the world have been without America defying other amazing powers that would have overwhelmed the world? What might the world be without American idea, and battle, and blood, and sacrifice?

- Without America would we live in a world without Democracy?

- Without America would we live in a world of continuing monarchies and kings and "divine rule"?

- Without America would we live in a world with a continuing slave trade?

- Without America would we live in a world with continuing Imperialism and Colonialism?

- Without America would we live in a world with continuing Nazism?

- Without America would we live in a world with continuing Communism?

- Without America would we live in a world with violent expanding Islamofascism?

?....?....?

Yeah, I thought so.

I don't need to specify every one of the extraordinary headways in science, disclosure, industry, medication, thinking, discovering that America and the American free-undertaking framework has created. Or on the other hand the subsequent exclusive expectation of living it spawned.

Sorry nonconformists, if not for America, a considerable lot of harmed philosophies would
rule the Earth today, and liberal illogical humanist fancy B.S. dreamland would not be somewhat imaginable. Any discussions of the "offenses" America has performed "from quite a while ago" become funny and become babble, as the present spoiled ruined nonconformists presumably would unquestionably have been squashed, disregarded, detained, devastated, subjugated, gassed, or killed off by any or those other ideologies.

I assume, America isn't genuinely awful now, is it?

To put down America, Liberals have to twist or distort History.

In contorting history, Students today are then ineffectively instructed in school, by deceitful Marxist "researchers" in academia.

Students these days will generally be shown more feeling than truth, and more educating of changed ideas of disappointment, than of ideas of traditionalism and success.

My past book, The Failure of Harvard – recounts this account of this disappointment of educating and of instructional method in the present schools and colleges. Especially Harvard.

How would I know this?

In the History Department at Harvard there are profiles of 50 History educators. In their profiles and books they have composed, 48 of 50 Harvard History educators tell the America detesting story.

After seeing this I ask, where are altogether the instructors recounting an America that is extraordinary and saved large number of lives?

They aren't there in light of the fact that Marxist and communist office heads didn't prescribe moderate point of view instructors to be employed. They needed to remove banter. They need to diviner the ideology.

My past book, The Failure of Harvard – recounts this account of this debasement, twisting, and disappointment of acumen, the disappointment of administration, and the disappointment of grant. Harvard schools of Math and Engineering are as yet authentic as there ARE right replies, or the structure will fall down.

Comprehensively, the Harvard History Department today is a FRAUD and

piggybacks its deceitful authenticity off its Science, Engineering, and Technology divisions. Humanities divisions have no such build, as numerous Humanities subjects depend on ONE individual's sentiments and feelings. Individuals with a similar point of view are recruited in progression making a mutilated perspective.

In Harvard Math, 2+2 is continually going to be 4… consistently. This is demonstrated, this is fact.

In Harvard History, particularly those that show Critical Race Theory, all white individuals are bigoted… Where is the confirmation that this is valid for every single one? How could this be estimated? Where is the observational proof and what is the logical verification of this?

Sounds like a "hypothesis" to me; a hypothesis to make dissention, division, character legislative issues, and at last push a Marxist agenda.

… . Deceitful scholarship.

If we are seeing certainties, we should analyze… . We should look for TRUTH!

As Ronald Reagan stressed over defying Marxism and its indecencies, he said that-

… ..some time or another when the opportunity arrives to convey the last final offer (from the Marxists), our acquiescence will be intentional, on the grounds that at that point we will have been debilitated from inside profoundly, ethically, and economically.
In this we should oppose – and retaliate with truths.
LIBERAL DEMOCRATS ARE THE NEW PLANTATION SLAVE MASTERS

During a House board of trustees declaration in 2019 regarding the matter of repayments for blacks for bondage over 150 years prior, an observer the Democrats thought may be well disposed, NFL Legend Burgess Owens, paralyzed the whole assembled crowd while during his declaration he said:

> *"I used to be a Democrat, until I did my set of experiences and discovered the wretchedness that that party brought to my race... We should pay restitution.*
> *How about the Democratic Party pay for all the hopelessness brought to my race..."*

WAIT! He just said what!?

It appears to be the Democrats, in attempting to utilize bigotry to isolate America, ran into somebody who did some schoolwork. Burgess Owens made a move to attack the Democratic Party "for all the wretchedness" they've brought to blacks; including things like the KKK and party's help of subjugation before the Civil War, to Jim Crow laws after the conflict, the wreck the downtown areas are in today with close to consistent Democratic coalition control.

Oh, gracious it appears as though the real truth is out in the open,

someone knows reality. That can't be great… . for the Democrats.

iberals and Democrats in government, the scholarly world, and in the media during this period decided not to take care of issues, however avoid their OWN FAILURES, and attempt and change the contention, and they vented their anger on then President Donald Trump.

It could be contended that Democrats have not been this irate at Republicans since Republicans and Abraham Lincoln liberated their slaves. The Democrats like slaves, since it makes a contracted elector base, where Democrats take from the working class and give cash to the obligated citizens and get the obligated electors to fault the working class as bigoted assuming they make any clamor concerning what the Democrats are doing. To Democrats, every individual who disagrees with them is a bigot, and those that need to free their elector slaves are even worse.

As numerous aircraft pilots know, the flack and fire coming from an adversary is the heaviest when you are straight over the target.

Donald Trump was liberal Democrats focus to divert from GENERATIONS of their disappointments... .Liberal disappointments in government, the scholarly world, and the media.

Democrats continually carry the demeanor to blacks, we will deal with you, we know what's best for you, we will give you free stuff and fault anything bad

on Republicans, or Trump allies, or Trump himself, by saying Trump is a bigot, as is each and every one of his allies, even the dark ones.

rump's dark allies are so bigoted truth be told, that they most likely stage KKK rallies.... . AGAINST THEMSELVES!

... definitely this B.S. account is disintegrating, as more African Americans displayed at Trump rallies, and after Trump were progressively casting a ballot Republican. Those damn, Black White supremacists!

et's get genuine, the Democrats have consistently been the bigots that needed to hold blacks down as it was in 1863 when REPUBLICAN President Abraham Lincoln, given the Emancipation Proclamation liberating the slaves.

epublicans have ALWAYS been the party "with the expectation of complimentary blacks", as Democrats have consistently been the "keep the Blacks contracted to us" party.

Going ahead after the Civil War it was clear the Democrats were on some unacceptable side of history in pretty much every milestone Civil Rights issues in the government.

• It was the DEMOCRATS that made and forced Jim Crow laws in the South after the Civil War.
• President Woodrow Wilson, a customary Southern-style DEMOCRAT from New Jersey, started isolation of administrative working environments in 1913.
• After the 1954 Brown versus Board choice, President Eisenhower, a REPUBLICAN sent government assembles to open schools for blacks when Democratic lead representatives and Democratic state legislators opposed him.
• The Civil Rights Act of 1964 80% of Republicans casted a ballot YES, and went against to Democrats where in their obstruction 40% casted a ballot NO.
• The Democrats were the party of Klansmen like Hillary coach Robert Byrd and segregationists like George Wallace....who got 13% of the decision in favor of President. Purported "bigoted Republicans" might have decided in favor of bigoted segregationist George Wallace... .they didn't – the Republican possibility for President won easily.After LBJ in the 1960's the Democrats technique to control blacks moved. Since they fell flat to hold blacks down with isolation and Jim Crow laws, and Democrat-accommodating gatherings like the KKK, the Democrats required another methodology for the control of blacks. Since Democrats couldn't

keep an iron grasp on their slaves any longer, they tried to control them in new ways with gifts and giveaways and become the "phony companion" Democrats. Control through dependency.

… Keep your companions close, keep your foes closer.

While the Republicans were lecturing autonomy and opportunity and freedom, the Democrats were lecturing a Marxist style free-stuff-for-all stage. Besides, Democrats attempted to condition blacks to make racial enmity and exploitation by making an "us against them" story. An exploitation the Democratic faction was generally dependable for!

Today this account converts into fundamental non-sensical assaults against ALL Republicans by dishonestly saying they are bigots, bigots, bigots, bigots. Indeed, the Democrats are liars, liars, liars, as they are slave drivers, slave drivers, slave masters.

Let's go a step further, lets really find out who the real racists are - Harvard or Republicans?

Let's see… ..Before REPUBLICAN President Abraham Lincoln liberated the slaves, most blacks needed to go abroad to acquire postgraduate educations. They couldn't get postgraduate educations at places like Harvard. In 1865: Patrick Francis Healy is the principal American dark to get a doctorate, procuring a Ph.D. from Louvain University… ..in Belgium.

We realize Democrats have consistently been bigots. They battled the Civil War to keep their slaves.

Democrats made and advanced Jim Crow.

Today Democrats use government cash and giveaways to keep up with command over blacks. Who were the last individuals from the KKK in Congress?..Democrats. Liberals today OWN every one of the chairman's workplaces and city gatherings in essentially every one of the significant urban communities, have people of color worked on in the 60 or 70 years they have been in charge? These Democrats are accountable for the cops, the spending plans, the schools.   As an outcome, there has not been a lot of progress in the lives of

blacks through giveaways and liberal policies.

Settled science, Democrats are the bigots holding blacks down. Conservatives and preservationists have consistently attempted to free individuals and secure their liberties.

Well, that is the Democrats, shouldn't something be said about Harvard's non-moderate bigot past?

- **In 1864 Republicans and Abraham Lincoln freed the slaves –** Harvard, it seems is behind the Republican lawmakers as it wasn't until **1869 that** George Lewis Ruffin is the first black to earn a degree from Harvard Law School **and in 1870**: Harvard

College FINALLY graduates its first black undergraduate student, Richard Theodore Greener.

- **Republicans passed the voting Rights Act of 1964** – Democrats tried to kill this legislation by an almost 2 to 1 margin…it wasn't until 1969 that Harvard FINALLY has its first tenured African American professor in Martin Kilson.
- **Republican President Donald Trump brings the lowest black unemployment rate ever and creates legislation that ends mass incarceration of all Americans** – Harvard instead hires black radicals in the humanities to fan the flames of the race wars. This is their evil methodology of continuing to control blacks and keep them dependant upon the government and the Democrats.

Liberals and Democrats and Harvard have consistently attempted to control blacks or hold them down. Until Republican enactment and activity incited them to make the best decision, Harvard played squarely into the racial divisions of this country.

For Harvard, their activities can legitimately be viewed as tokenisim, or opposite prejudice, responsibility, or generally malicious of all - fanning the flares of racial difficulty, by pushing and advancing a disdain powered gathering personality exploitation account. Besides, Harvard just appears to pass judgment on individuals by its skin tone or gathering personality than their acumen or character, as Harvard dismissed the top individuals of the WRONG ethnic minority by dismissing Asian understudies in the 2010's to acknowledge less competent understudies from other identifier and qualifier gatherings. Harvard was sued and didn't care.

What about Harvard's ideological racism?

Liberals own downtown. For what reason are these spots a harsh and ineffectively drove third world country into themselves? Where was the expectation and change? Liberals have been in charge of the Mayors office and city boards all things considered large urban communities in America for quite a long time. At times, moving toward 100 years! We just had 8 years of a dark President and well disposed Attorney Generals. For what reason is the downtown still a mess?

Maybe in light of the fact that the exhaustive Liberal-Democratic-Harvard philosophy is an all out failure.

It is currently clear the new ranch is presently downtown and the Liberal-Democrats-Harvard the scholarly world own it.

hy hasn't Harvard in the entirety of their scholarly brightness stood in opposition to this?

Harvard is one of the many schools that conformed to making a crumbling condition in downtown by obliging business ideas and belief systems that sent all the blue collar positions abroad to places like China. It was approaches like this that annihilated the average workers in America, especially blacks.

Somehow Harvard likewise is one of the platitude extreme left foundations of disdain and complaint that abhors all Republicans that consistently needed to free their slaves, and specifically Donald Trump, who does things like make responsibilities to get dark joblessness down to its least levels of all time. Pandering philosophical bigoted liars at places like Harvard need to keep blacks attached to the public authority and dependent.

hey need to keep those downtown schools a debacle, and a disorderly mess.

The Liberal-Democrat-Harvard bigots need Blacks to have annihilated families where 70% of children are conceived out of wedlock.

Republicans and Trump need blacks to be free, blacks don't need presents or to be controlled, they need their families back, they need their own positions and the regard that accompanies all of those!

acist Harvard assumes in any case, as some way or another, they the Democrats

and liberal world class know better.... sounds pretty manor expert to me.

Furthermore, places like Harvard advance liberal all out social crazy situation and disorder, which prompts a blast in wrongdoing and at last lead America to a program of mass imprisonment. Conservatives and Trump defied this messed up mass imprisonment and followed isolating out peaceful wrongdoers to liberated from the cycle, to break the Liberal-Democratic-Harvard pattern of the American Education to Incarceration complex.

HARVARD AND ALL OF MARXIST ACADEMIA NEED TO STOP WITH THE LIES

Harvard, in pushing Marxist belief systems and "hypotheses" are a lot of cultural annihilating Marxists that can't recount to the best story at any point told, and they ought to be supplanted or basically be brought to balance.

The best story at any point told is that of America!

So quite a bit of the present extreme left liberal scholarly community "history" (their verifiable viewpoint) is from an "everybody is a casualty" mentality. Indeed, I recount the tale of how carrying on with life as a human is a battle unto itself FOR ALL PEOPLE IN ALL NATIONS. I recount the tale of how life itself is a battle, and how Americans sublimely accomplished significance and saved the world.

I mean assuming we are truly going to recount the narrative of all that is dreadful in America lets recount the terrible story of nonconformists here in America.

- Liberals give away atomic bomb secrets to the Soviets that fueled the Cold War.
- Liberals looked the other way and covered up for Marxists when Marxists were killing millions, and imprisoning millions of people in places like Russia, China, and Cambodia, way more than Hitler ever did. This is YOUR legacy liberals.
- Liberals also promote the glorification of drugs and drug culture that helps create demand and fuels the Drug and narco-wars south of the border that kills tens of thousands and sends waves of refugees fleeing the murder liberals create.
- Liberals continuously attack families and create and push a dark

  social of skepticism and moral relativism, prompting wretchedness, suicides and anxiety.
- Liberals have had total control over the inner cities power structure for a really long time keeping blacks and minorities in destitution and darkness.

Two can play that character game dissidents… . anyway our own has an establishment of truth, yours an establishment of feeling and distortion.

… and you dim and abhorrent dissidents presently can't seem to make up for your many, many sins. We are coming for YOUR sculptures and YOUR organizations… me giving it to the morons at Harvard, in my book The Failure of Harvard, is only the start of the fightback.

TRUTH CANNOT BE STOPPED

hen genuine Americans today stand up and challenge the harmed liberal universality and the socially sensitive hogwash that has completely tainted the scholarly world today, they are proceeding with the tradition of battle against horrendous philosophies our progenitors faced.

Free-for-all, everything-goes-and-nothing-matters, skeptical Liberal Democrats are sincerely accepting things very little not quite the same as Communism, and will be crushed, as far as we might be concerned has consistently been unfeasible and will at last implode in on itself or be overthrown.

People that realize the American history realize that the best of America and conventional American qualities merit recalling, merit saving, merit ensuring, merit celebrating, and ARE, for sure, worth battling for. As this is us, and this is of our innate character.

America isn't generally a beautiful story of simple triumph, and government assistance checks for all from support to grave. America isn't for a lot of ruined inheritant kids hoping to waste their ancestors' persistent effort for an existence of degeneracy and relaxation. America, as every age discovers is for those that need it, will work for it, and need a shot at accomplishing their fantasies and of progress regardless of how unobtrusive or how great.

Today, we see the continuous and ceaseless battle still. Donald Trump is

one of numerous Americans that battles this battle, and that is the reason dissidents HATE him. Nonconformists and the media and the scholarly community loathed Reagan as well, and both George Bushes, and Republican Presidential competitors Bob Dole, and John McCain, and Mitt Romney.

Now that dissidents, the scholarly community, and the media have made a response to their rule of fear, the Trump administration, they are presently uncovered. The Trump administration turned into a battle to set out freedom that got more diligently in America because of awful economic alliance, awful schools, distorted corporate valuations, harmful social qualities moving from Hollywood, free gifts and trillions in shortfalls, and ineffectively politically considered and executed wars.

As the Trump administration finished dissidents to recover control currently have to CENSOR, CENSOR EVERYTHING

> CENSOR reality. Edit
> their disappointments.
> Edit their delusion.
> CENSOR all contradiction (valid or not)
> CENSOR to ensure their authoritarian control of media and social
> media.

CENSOR the way that so large numbers of these individuals don't have the answer for our concerns yet are truth be told just making more problems.

t has for some time been valid throughout hundreds of years that restriction normally emerges out to secure a wrecked decision class. This is the reason America had the First Amendment.

True Americans have tried to ensure Constitutional qualities INCLUDING FREE SPEECH. This to bring to the light of day, defilement and brokenness to deliver a superior country for our kids. With values like this, America through its set of experiences, has enlivened, has accomplished, has saved the world consistently from oppression, from defilement, and from horrendous belief systems that look to obliterate all that is great. Tragically, presently it appears to be those foes are assaulting from the inside and have the logo CNN on their mouthpieces. They esteem their right to speak freely, despite the fact that such a great deal it is untruths and twisting, while at the same time sitting around while others are silenced.

thus, the solution for control is all the more free speech.

The battle for our best has been a continuous battle, and a battle it has been.

As Ronald Reagan once broadly said –

> *You and I have a meeting with predetermination. We can protect for
> our kids this, the last best any desire for man on the planet, or we*

can condemn them to venture out into 1,000 years of dimness. In case we come up short, basically let our kids and our kids' youngsters say of us we supported our concise second here. We did everything that can possibly be done.

As our Children and GenZ foster point of view, they will perceive how the extreme left and some narrow minded Boomers gave a valiant effort to obliterate GenX and Millennials, financially, profoundly, and inwardly. The youthful will see this and start to renounce a significant part of the extreme left belief system and narcissistic qualities that helped the accident of 2008 occur, and perpetually wars occur, and the declining future, and expanded paces of nervousness and wretchedness and medication use in their elderly folks… .and see the love seat so many of them live on in their parent's cellars into their 30's.

hey will realize it isn't all their issue. Their "trendy" scholarly, media, and political pioneers bombed them, as they buckled down additional time to kill off Trump and tried to control his allies, preservationists, and even centrists.

The offspring of today will hear from their grandparents, accounts of Americas past and a superior time, a more prosperous time, and how it was botched, wasted, and taken from them.
Truth, Perspective, and making it right is the test of all generations.

As those youngsters, close or more than 30, were headed to their parent's love seats, most by no shortcoming of their own, they can consider the potential that America presented before, and how today is neither as financially nor as profoundly however encouraging as it seemed to be in the past.

How they stand up to this is their meeting with their American predetermination.